The Concise Guide
to
the Waterfalls
of Iceland

Michael Kendall-Tobias

As author of The Concise Guide to the Waterfalls of Iceland, I am both a contributor to, and user of, worldwaterfalldatabase.com. Some of the data in this book are reproduced with the kind permission of the authors of worldwaterfalldatabase.com.

The contents of The Concise Guide to the Waterfalls of Iceland are selected from, and an abbreviated version of, A Guide to the Waterfalls of Iceland, by the same author.

I have made every attempt to ensure that the facts, figures and descriptions in this guide are as accurate as possible. However, this guide is a personal work, so much of the information is subjective and either impossible to quantify or verify, or has eluded my best efforts to check it. So please bear this in mind when, inevitably, you question some of what you read. Should you wish to contact me regarding any information in this guide you can do so at aguidetothewaterfallsoficeland@gmail.com.

Finally, I am indebted to Robert Simpson for his invaluable time spent proofreading this work. He has seen what I could not see and his corrections and suggestions have both improved this guide and raised it to a higher professional standard and a more enjoyable read.

Introduction

Iceland is said to be the land of over 10,000 waterfalls. This amounts to about one waterfall for every 10 square kilometres, which makes Iceland the most densely such covered country on Earth. With so many it is hardly surprising that Iceland can boast of some of the most beautiful waterfalls in the world. This book is a guide to over 100 of those waterfalls, with references to about 150.

So are these the best falls in Iceland? That is not a question that is easily answered. They may not be the highest waterfalls, nor the widest. The falls in this guide have been selected based on a combination of their overall scenic beauty (their 'wow' factor) and their accessibility. For example, you will not find the tallest waterfall in Iceland, Morsárfoss, which is practically unreachable. Neither will you find all the falls that appear on Icelandic road maps. While you may assume that if a waterfall is named on a road map then it must really be worth seeing, this is surprisingly not the case. It is one of the enigmas of Icelandic cartography that many of the most breath-taking falls are not on the maps, while many others of only marginal touristic significance are. In this book you will find not only the most visited waterfalls in Iceland but also some that are undoubtedly not very high, nor wide, but are so fascinating, in such lovely, scenic settings, and so easy to reach, they deserve a visit.

In particular there are five important waterfall hikes: Forsæludalur, Seyðisfjörður, Laugarfell, Skaftafell and Skóga, that are fully described with details of each significant waterfall along the trail.

Conventions

There are many conventions used throughout this book that should be explained to facilitate your understanding of the information presented. They are listed below.

Order of listing

Waterfalls are presented as if travelling from Reykjavik in a clockwise spiral, first heading north-west, then north and along the north coast to the east, then along the southern coastal area going west, and finishing up in the southern central and highland area. There are several instances in this guide of clusters of waterfalls located close together or along the same river, usually visited as a group. In these cases, the major heading is the group name and the individual falls are listed as secondary headings.

Spelling

Icelandic spelling is used for all Icelandic names. The Icelandic alphabet is a Latin alphabet that includes some letters duplicated with acute accents (á, é, í, ó, ú, ý) or an umlaut (ö), and the ligature æ. In addition, it includes two distinctive letters: eth (Ð,ð) transliterated on most English and other Western European keyboards by D,d, and the runic letter thorn (Þ,þ) transliterated by Th,th, and pronounced like 'th' in the word 'thin'. (However, Ð is pronounced similarly to the 'th' in the word 'father', and so should possibly be transliterated more accurately by Th.)

Most Icelandic place names have endings that describe their geological features, thus these can be used as an aid in understanding the nature underlying the Icelandic names in this guide. The list below covers the most important place name suffixes:

Suffix	Landscape Feature	Suffix	Landscape Feature
á	River	jökull	Glacier
ás	Small hill	jökullsá	Glacial river
bakki	River bank	kvísl	River or river branch
brekka	Slope	lækur	Small stream or brook
bunga	Rounded mountain top	lón	Lagoon
dalur	Valley	melur	Barren or stony plain
fell	Fell, mountain or hill	múli	Headland
Fjall	Mountain	öræfi	Desert
fjörður	Fjord	skagi	Peninsula
fljót	Large river	skarð	Mountain pass
foss	Waterfall	skögur	Woodland
fossar	Series of waterfalls	tunga	Tongue of land
gil	Gorge or ravine	vatn	Lake
heiði	Heath or moor	vegur	Road
hvoll	Hill	völlur	Plain (plural: vellir)

Name

Many waterfalls have two or more names, and it is not always clear which is the best name to use. One name may appear on a map while the signpost on the road has a different name. A name may be on a past land survey but has since fallen into disuse. In other cases the local population may use a different name to the official one. A good example is Gljúfurafoss. Gljúfurárfoss or Gljúfrabúi are commonly used alternative names for this waterfall, but the locals often call it Hamragarðafoss after the ancient farmstead Hamragarðar on which land it is situated. Then there is the renowned Dynjandi in the Westfjords which is also known as Fjallfoss, or Dynjandifoss, or even Dynjandafoss. Waterfalls in this guide are listed by their most commonly used names and include their other aliases.

In a country with over 10,000 waterfalls, you can expect more than a few to be unnamed, and many more where the name is unknown by anyone other than the locals. Surprisingly, there are even some well-known falls that have never been given names, despite the passing of years and the increasingly frequent visits by enthusiastic hikers and waterfall lovers. So do not be surprised to see a waterfall listed as 'Unknown' (by the author), it can still be a lovely waterfall.

Location and Region

Each waterfall entry includes a small outline map of Iceland marked with a star to show the location of the falls (or group of falls) described. This provides an immediate understanding of approximately where the waterfall is situated.

This guide is based on a convention of eight geographical regions, plus an extra sub-region. Since the Southern Region covers not only the populated south coast but much of central Iceland and the touristic areas of the highlands, from the perspective of a touring guide it makes sense to separate the southern central areas from the rest. So the Southern Region, Suðurland, has been split into a Southern Coastal Region and Southern Central Region. There are no waterfalls worthy of mention in the Southern Peninsula, Suðurnes, so there are seven geographical regions covered in this guide. They are:

Icelandic name	Interpretation
Höfuðborgarsvæði	Capital Region
Vesturland	Western Region
Vestfirðir	Westfjords Region
Norðurland vestra	North-western Region
Norðurland eystra	North-eastern Region
Austurland	Eastern region
Suðurland	Southern Coastal Region and Southern Central Region

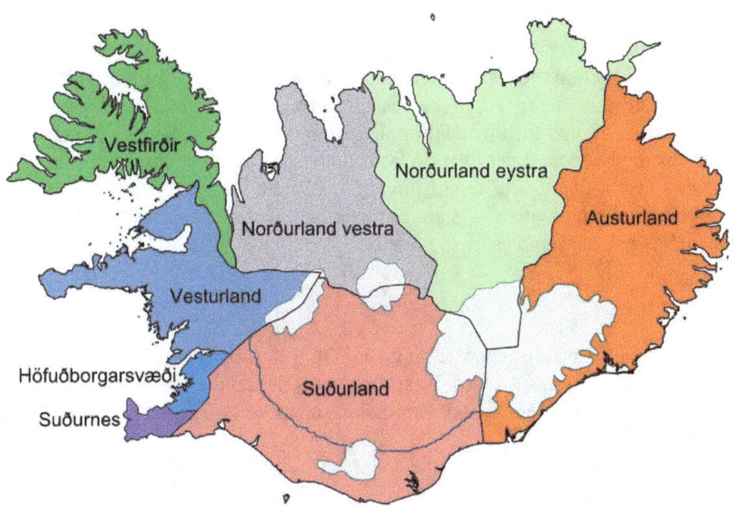

The eight geographical regions of Iceland. The Southern region, Suðurland, is shown divided into a coastal sub-region and central sub-region.

Town

This is the closest major city or town to the waterfall. Due to the sparse population density of Iceland, it can sometimes be quite a few kilometres away. For the same reason, the size of the town can be very variable and often closer to that of a village in other parts of the world.

Area

This describes the area in which the waterfall is located. It is usually a valley but may sometimes be a heath or the name of the fjord into which the river flows.

River

The name of the watercourse is provided. Usually this is the river, or stream, that the waterfall sits within, but occasionally it is the river the waterfall runs into if the source is a lake or porous ground.

GPS

The GPS coordinates, longitude and latitude, are provided for each waterfall. These are given in both conventional degrees/minutes/seconds and decimal degrees formats. Each waterfall photograph has the GPS coordinates of the position at which it was taken. These can often be more useful than the coordinates of the waterfall itself when navigating to the desired viewpoint.

A note of warning, for directions, it is tempting to rely entirely on a GPS navigation system using the coordinates of the waterfall, but in the case of waterfalls located some distance from the main roads, the system may lead you down an erroneous route to the wrong side of a waterfall. For example, you may be led on a 50 km detour round to the south bank of a waterfall, when there is a dirt road that takes you close to the north bank just 5 km away. Use the waterfall's GPS coordinates with caution, or better still use the coordinates given for the location of one of the photographs of the falls.

Facing

This is the compass direction the waterfall faces, which is not necessarily that of the river it is on or runs into. A waterfall facing east receives the morning sunlight. Sometimes it will have multiple tiers (see below) that turn when dropping from one to the other, for instance the top tier may face south while the second tier turns to face south-west. In other cases a waterfall may have multiple sections, each facing a different direction. In both instances there is range of facing directions, so this is denoted with a '-' sign. For example, Goðafoss forms a wide horseshoe that faces N-E, which is not the same as facing due NE.

Tiers

This is number of major steps or ledges composing the waterfall. It is usually only one but there are several with four tiers or more. Occasionally, the falls descend a convoluted incline or tumble of rocks and the number of tiers is indeterminable, in these rare cases the number of tiers is denoted as 'Multiple'.

Ratings

This guide rates each waterfall on height, width and scenic beauty. Ratings, in stars, are purely subjective and are based on a point system, in half point increments. Why not a broader full point system? Because the use of many points gives the illusion of precision, whereas due to the very subjective nature of the evaluations I believe that only a limited scale is realistic. A half point denotes an uncertainty in evaluation, so that 3½ points means 'I'm not really sure if this is a 2 or a 3, it depends'.

Why the uncertainty? First, because in many if not most cases the dimensions are not listed in any documentation and have been judged by eye, with no measuring equipment, and therefore can be very inaccurate. Second, because in Iceland the amount of water in a river and waterfall varies tremendously with the time of year and weather. Even an accurate measurement at one time may be many metres different from a measurement at a different time. For a small waterfall the variation can be immense. A waterfall with a height of 1 m and width of 3 m in early spring when the river is in full flood may have the inverse measurements of 1 m width and 3 m height in late summer when drying up — a variation of 300%. Unless the waterfall is officially measured over an extended period, the average waterfall height and width will be unknown. Even documented figures can vary significantly. The famous Skogafoss is quoted by some sources as having a height of about 70 m and width of 30 m, and in others as having a height of 60 m and width of 25 m. In the rating system, Skogafoss would get a rating a 5 for height and 3½ for width. Where there are known height and width measurements these are included. Where there are multiple tiers the different heights are shown separated by a '+' sign. A range in reported heights or widths is denoted with a '-' sign.

Height and width: The roughly logarithmic seven-point scales are for the total height and width of the falls from topmost brink to lowermost basin. The rating increases one point for each approximate doubling in height or width. This system is used since, visually, it is far more meaningful than a linear scale.

Total height (m)	Rating	Total width (m)	Rating
<=2	0	<=2	0
<=5	1	<=5	1
<=12	2	<=12	2
<=25	3	<=25	3
<=50	4	<=50	4
<=100	5	<=100	5
>100	6	>100	6

Scenery: A six-point scale measures the visual impact of the total scene. A mediocre waterfall in terms of height and width can be magnificent in the right setting. Similarly two very different falls can have the same overall scenic beauty. Háifoss is over 100 m high but only about 12 m wide, while Goðafoss is only about 12 m high but over 100 m wide. Háifoss pours down into a beautiful canyon and Goðafoss spans the river in a horseshoe shape of four sections. Both are breath-taking waterfalls.

Scenery	Rating
Unremarkable	0
Pretty, picturesque	1
Lovely, delightful	2
Beautiful, elegant	3
Wonderful, magnificent, marvellous	4
Stupendous, awesome, breath-taking	5

Access

Many roads in Iceland do not permit two-wheel-drive (2WD) vehicles. You need a four-wheel-drive vehicle (4WD) to drive on mountain roads, classified as F-roads. This means that some waterfalls are only accessible by 4WD. The Icelandic government is rapidly improving the road system and what is an F-road today may become a standard road for regular vehicles in the near future. The pace of road building has given rise to many roads that are still designated as F-roads but are quite accessible by high ground clearance 2WD SUV (Sports Utility Vehicle) type cars. Sometimes only a short stretch of good F-road is all that stops a 2WD car from reaching its destination, so this guide introduces an SUV classification. Consider an SUV rating as an easy 4WD road or a very bumpy 2WD road for high clearance vehicles only. This is not a category recognised by Iceland or any insurance companies, and taking an SUV on an F-road, even a very good F-road, is at your own uninsured risk.

Many touristic adventure companies in Iceland use what are termed 'Super Jeeps', with gigantic tyres and extremely high ground clearance. Most of the time, such vehicles are not necessary during the summer months, even on non-classified dirt tracks, except in bad weather and high flood conditions, although they do afford a greater speed, margin of safety, and comfort, not to mention tourist appeal. None of the waterfalls in this guide require a Super Jeep for access.

This guide rates the primary accessibility for each waterfall as 2WD, SUV or 4WD. Secondary accessibility is based on the walking distance and how long it takes an average, middle-aged person to reach the waterfall. Unless the trail is a loop, you will need to double these distances and times for the full return trip. Most of the waterfalls in this guide have ratings of Drive-up and Easy.

Rating	Distance (km)	Time (hr)	Explanation
Drive-up	0	0	There is parking very close to the waterfall and only a few metres to walk, usually on a well-defined path.
Easy	<=2	0.5	It is a short easy walk to the waterfall for anybody except the infirm.
Moderate	<=4	1	Be prepared to spend a little effort. The walk is either a few easy kilometres, or a little steep or rough.
Vigorous	<=8	2	A good hike, a fair distance, possibly over some rough terrain. You will enjoy it.
Strenuous	<=16	4	About a day's hike there and back, for serious hikers. It's probably worth it though.
Tough	>16	>4	For the adventurous and fit when the hike may be more important than the destination

Many waterfalls are on farmland and therefore on private property, but this doesn't mean that access is barred. Mass tourism is a fairly recent phenomenon for Iceland and until now there hasn't been a real need for strict regulation of the rights of way to waterfalls or other attractions on private property. Consequently, the law is hazy about what is permissible and what isn't. In general, there is a rule of free access to natural sites, but this comes with certain common sense, if not legal, caveats.

- Land with buildings, crops, horses, or cattle are deemed private and no trespassing is allowed.
- Privately built and maintained roads may be barred with or without a gate at the discretion of the owner.
- When a public road is barred by a locked gate, vehicles are not permitted but hikers may climb over.
- When a public road is barred by an unlocked gate, a vehicle or person can go through the gate, taking care to leave it in the state in which it was found.
- When a trail is barred by a fence, sometimes barbed or electrified, hikers may climb over.
- Lastly, the trail to some sites may require crossing close to a farmyard, or other property near to a working area. These are the most difficult to access, so if in doubt ask the owner. Most farmers will gladly give permission to hikers to traverse their property – but usually not for motorised vehicles.

Description

Interesting diverse information about the waterfall is presented in this section. It may be related to the location, size and volume of the falls and river, or to historical legends.

Directions

Directions to each waterfall are provided, usually starting from a major town off Route 1 or other main highway. These should enable you to get to the waterfall itself or to a suitable viewpoint without having to rely on the GPS coordinates. The road or route names are also given, since Icelanders usually refer to these names rather than the numbers.

Directions and advice are also provided for the walk or hike from the parking area to the prime viewing location.

This section also provides any notable difficulties and useful tips for getting the best out of your trip.

Kermóafoss (Skorarhylsfoss)

Region:	Höfuðborgarsvæði	Facing:	NW	
Town:	Reykjavik	Tiers:	1	
Area:	Elliðaárdalur	Height:	★ ½	
River:	Elliðaá	Width:	★ ★ ★	
GPS:	64°06'57.1" N 21°49'28.7" W	Scenery:	★ ★ ★	
(deg dec)	64.115856, -21.824630	Access:	2WD	Easy

Description

You might not think that there could be any waterfalls in Reykjavik but you would be mistaken. There are several pretty cascades around a very pleasant trail within Reykjavik's underappreciated local recreational area. The park, located in the valley of Elliðaárdalur, is a lush oasis of calm, well worth taking the time to explore. The river Elliðaá flows through it, splitting into two branches that are separated by a lovely woodland with criss-crossing footpaths for joggers, hikers and families out for a relaxing walk. The main 5 km circular Fraeðslustigur trail is paved. The Elliðaá is a salmon river and although it might seem incongruous, right on Reykjavik's urban doorstep, it is well-populated with salmon that you may be lucky enough to see.

There are four noteworthy waterfalls in the park:

- Sjávarfoss
- Búrfoss
- Arnarfoss
- Kermóafoss

Other waterfalls are:

- Skötufoss
- Selásfoss
- Ullarfoss
- Breiðholtsfoss

Kermóafoss, or Skorarhylsfoss according to the information panel, is a very picturesque waterfall of multiple tiers and channels falling over one another over a drop of some 5 m. Though the falls are not spectacularly high, the overall scene, with the beautiful woodland and vegetation, is one which makes you stop and spend a while absorbing it all. This waterfall is well worth a trip to the park, but do walk through the woodland and appreciate its charm while you are there.

Directions

Although there are several entrances to the park and several walking routes, this guide proposes the following starting point. From Reykjavik, take Route 49 (Nesbraut) going east, and pass junction 49/41. Route 41 is Reykjanesbraut. (On a GPS, Route 49 may be shown as Artunsbrekka or Vesturlandsvegur). Immediately take the first exit down to a T-junction then turn left and park. There is an information panel nearby showing the park and trails around it.

Follow the yellow trail anticlockwise along the bike path, going first across a footbridge over the river. You will pass Sjávarfoss, Búrfoss and Arnarfoss. Kermóafoss is just beyond the southern end of the trail, marked in yellow on the signs. You can easily see it as you cross the footbridge over the west branch of the river to get to the east branch for the return part of the walk, and it is only about 100 m further upriver.

You can also see the rapids Ullarfoss and Skötufoss on the east branch as you head back up to the parking area. If you are in need of greater exercise, there are two other waterfalls in the park, Selásfoss and Breiðholtsfoss, but they are considerably further to the south.

Kermóafoss is about 5 m high, with multiple tiers and channels, in a beautiful setting. GPS: 64°6'56" N 21°49'32" W (64.11556, -21.82556)

Búrfoss is located at the north end of the trail. It is a pleasant spot for a picnic. GPS: 64°7'16" N 21°50'46" W (64.12111, -21.84611)

Oxarárfoss

Region:	Suðurland (coastal)	Facing:	SE		
Town:	Mosfellsbær	Tiers:	2		
Area:	Þingvellir	Height:	★★★	11+2 m	
River:	Öxará	Width:	★★	6 m	
GPS:	64°15'56.8" N 21°07'04.2" W	Scenery:	★★★ ½		
(deg dec)	64.265781, -21.117840	Access:	2WD	Easy	

Description

Öxarárfoss is within Þingvellir National Park. The river Öxará falls over a cliff into a valley formed by the separation of the North Atlantic and Eurasian continents. The first tier forms a curtain of about 11 metres by 6 metres then there is a much broader two-meter drop. Below the waterfall the river turns 90° to the south-west, flowing down the impressive Almannagjá gorge formed by the rift, then over another cliff to the valley below. The geology of the surroundings is dramatic, forming a very scenic frame to the falls themselves.

The site is along the so-called touristic 'Golden Circle', and is one of the most popular destinations in Iceland, so you can expect to encounter crowds during the summer months. Due to the falls' south-eastern orientation, and to have some degree of solitude, you should view Öxarárfoss in the early morning. There is a wooden viewing platform at the falls, and a good deal of spray.

Directions

From Reykjavik, take Route 1 north to Hvalfjörður and Mosfellsbær. Then take Route 36 (Þingvallavegur) and follow the signs to Þingvellir. Öxarárfoss is 2.5 km north-east of the Þingvellir visitor centre. Turn off Route 36 to a signposted car park just for the falls, then walk about 1 km on a sometimes rocky path to the base of the waterfall. Alternatively, you can walk 1.7 km from the visitor centre along a pleasant trail.

Öxarárfoss in the spray. GPS: 64°15'56.6" N 21°7'1.7" W (64.265722, -21.117139)

Glymur (Glymurfoss)

Region:	Vesturland	Facing:	S	
Town:	Grundarhverfi	Tiers:	1	
Area:	Hvalfjörður	Height:	★ ★ ★ ★ ★ ★	198 m
River:	Botnsá	Width:	★ ★ ★ ★	
GPS:	64°23'27.7" N 21°15'07.1" W	Scenery:	★ ★ ★ ★ ★	
(deg dec)	64.391021, -21.251981	Access:	2WD	Strenuous

Description

Glymur originates from a small lake within a fairly flat plain. Over the millennia, the Botnsá has dropped over the lip of a cliff and carved out a deep slot that is nearly a kilometre in length and well over 200 m deep. It is one of the few waterfalls (along with others such as Beljandi, Dynjandi, Dýnkur, Granni, Gjallandi, Neffji, Rjúkandi and Skinandi) that are known by names that do not end in 'foss' or 'fossar'. The word 'Glymur' can be roughly translated as 'crashing' or 'roaring', and no doubt the name comes from the sound it makes as it plunges down into that astonishingly deep, narrow chasm.

Glymur is Iceland's second highest waterfall, with a recorded height of 198 m. However, the measurement of the width is open to many interpretations. Although the river in the canyon is only about 10 wide, Glymur is considerably larger. The main stream is a narrow horsetail, but the remaining water fans out and drops over the ledge at various points forming a veil type waterfall of up to about 40 m. Considering the whole flow, the maximum spread can be over 100 m wide.

Directions

Take Route 47 (Hvalfjarðarvegur) going eastwards to the very end of Hvalfjörður bay. After crossing a bridge turn east on the signposted road to 'Glymur Foss'. Follow the road for 0.75 km then take the easily missed sharp left turn. Continue for another 3 km to the parking area for Glymur.

Although it is only about 4 km to the top of Glymur it is a strenuous hike and requires some agility. The trail starts at the parking area by passing through a gate and following a gravel path. Yellow-painted rocks mark the route. After about 250 m the path forks into an easier northern trail that then follows the western side of the canyon, and a harder southern trail that then follows the eastern side. Most people take the tougher one since it affords the best views. The first 1.25 km are deceptively easy, but then the trail seems to stop just before reaching the gorge. At this point it makes a sharp left bend and disappears into a low, dark cave before emerging and heading to the river below. You will need to scramble a bit to climb down some rocks.

You then follow the river a short distance before having to cross it using stepping-stones and a narrow log with a cable handrail. You will need to duck under the cable at the halfway point. After crossing the river, the trail climbs very steeply with various muddy, rocky and scree areas, often with narrow paths and steep drops to the side. Ropes are provided at several points for you to haul yourself up – you will need them. At one point, the trail passes a small tributary waterfall with a sheltered pool.

The first view of the falls is after about 1.75 km where the trail becomes steeper, and the best views are at about 2.5 and 2.75 km. The final 500 m are the steepest. Depending on your fitness and stops to admire the view, the hike there and back will take you between 2 and 4 hours.

At the top you can cross the river above the waterfall and hike down on the western side. You will have to wade across the Botnsá since there is no footbridge over this part of the river.

On your way to Glymur, or on the way back you might want to stop and take a look at Mígandi, a small waterfall next to the parking area at the entrance to the road leading to Glymur. Also, from there, you can go to Paradísarfoss, which, descends 30 m in five tiers, within an interesting rocky gorge. Getting to the viewpoint involves scrambling up along the tree line from the path leading to Mígandi, then to the edge of the gorge. Once there, it is a beautiful view looking down and up to the top of the falls.

Glymur in its 198 m of glory. GPS: 64°23'16.7" N 21°15'18.9" W (64.387968, -21.255259)

Hraunfossar (Hraunfoss)

Region:	Vesturland	Facing:	S	
Town:	Reykholt	Tiers:	1	
Area:	Borgarfjörður, Hálsasveit	Height:	★★	12 m
River:	Hvítá	Width:	★★★★★	
GPS:	64°42'09.5" N 20°58'52.2" W	Scenery:	★★★★	
(deg dec)	64.702639, -20.981167	Access:	2WD	Drive-up

Description

Although signposted as being in Borgarfjörður, Hraunfossar is some way inland, in the area of Hálsasveit. It is one Iceland's most unusual waterfalls since it does not stem from any river or lake. 'Hraunfossar' means 'Lava waterfalls'. The water seeps, seemingly magically, from between the rocks of the Hallmundar lava field, then runs down into the river Hvítá below. The so-called 'width', is in this case the length parallel to the river, and is about 200 m, but taking into account all the smaller springs down the gorge can amount to several hundred metres. The height varies over this tremendous width, with the tallest section producing the most flow. Hraunfossar is also exceptional for its colours. The white, lacy streamers of the emanating waters contrast beautifully with the green vegetation, dark lava, and the turquoise-blue water of the Hvítá.

Directions

Hraunfossar is east of Reykholt. From Route 1, take Route 50 (Dragavegur) east to Reykholt then take Route 518 (Hálsasveitarvegur) for about 23 km. Follow the signposts for Hraunfossar and park in the designated parking area.

Because of the popularity of the site, there is a well-managed parking area and boardwalk that connects the prominent viewpoints, the first of these is adjacent to the car park. There are also some simple tourist facilities and toilets near the car park.

Hraunfossar seeps out of the Hallmundar lava field. GPS: 64°42'8" N 20°58'40" W (64.70222, -20.97778)

Barnafoss (Bjarnafoss)

Region:	Vesturland	Facing:	NW	
Town:	Reykholt	Tiers:	1	
Area:	Borgarfjörður, Hálsasveit	Height:	★ ★	9 m
River:	Hvítá	Width:	★ ★	11 m
GPS:	64°42'06.5" N 20°58'24.6" W	Scenery:	★ ★ ½	
(deg dec)	64.701792, -20.973496	Access:	2WD	Easy

Description

Barnafoss is the neighbour to the much more interesting Hraunfossar. The Hvítá forms the falls as it sluices through a narrow gorge carved into a lava flow, with a more vertical section of the falls being found near the top, and shallower cascades toward the bottom. At the foot of the falls the river dives beneath at least one natural bridge or, rather, a portion of a collapsed lava tube. This area is visible from the major viewpoints. The main part of the falls is unfortunately hidden in the gorge around the corner. It should be at least partially visible from further upstream, but on the south side the area is signposted as prohibited. However, you can view it from the rocky path on the north side.

Barnafoss translates to 'Children's Falls'. The name comes from a story that tells of two local boys who were told to stay at home while their parents went to church with their ploughman for Christmas mass. The boys grew bored and decided to follow their parents by taking a shortcut across a natural rock bridge above the waterfall. In crossing, they fell into the river, never to be seen again. Their mother, distraught, had the bridge destroyed so nobody else would suffer the same fate. A variation of the story is that the mother put a spell on the bridge saying that nobody would ever cross it without drowning, and an earthquake later destroyed the arch.

Directions

Follow the directions for Hraunfossar. From the parking area, follow the boardwalk east, past Hraunfossar, for about 200 m to the bridge crossing the Hvítá. There is a managed path to the south of the river, and a short, rocky trail on the north side, over the bridge.

Barnafoss, viewed from the bridge over the Hvítá, looking north. Note the viewing platform in the picture, to get an idea of scale. GPS: 64°42'7" N 20°58'28" W (64.70194, -20.97444)

Glanni

Region:	Vesturland		Facing:	SW	
Town:	Borganes		Tiers:	2	
Area:	Norðurárdalur		Height:	★★	8 m
River:	Norðurá		Width:	★★★★	
GPS:	64°45'13.0" N 21°32'45.8" W		Scenery:	★★★★ ½	
(deg dec)	64.753618, -21.546044		Access:	2WD	Easy

Description

Glanni is a magnificent though relatively less well-known waterfall, whether in full flood in spring or when the rocks are at their most visible in late summer. The name is unusual in that it does not end in 'foss' – it means 'a reckless person', but the history behind the name is unknown.

Glanni has three main chutes descending in two tiers, with an intermediate island most easily visible at low water levels. Its width is around 50 m depending on the water level, and it has a fish ladder looping round on the north side. The positions of the rocks channel the river so that it surges and swirls on its way down, creating ever-changing shapes that fascinate the eye and capture the attention. A waterfall not to miss.

Directions

Glanni is located off Route 1, south of Bifröst. Coming from Borganes, go about 30 km northeast and take the road on the right signposted Glanni-Paradis. Park in the golf course parking area and take the path on the right for 300 m to a large viewing platform looking down on the waterfall.

The swirling water can hold your attention for a long time. GPS: 64°45'13" N 21°32'52" W (64.75361, -21.54778)

Svöðufoss

Region:	Vesturland	Facing:	N	
Town:	Ólafsvik	Tiers:	2	
Area:	Hólsdalur	Height:	★★★	
River:	Hólmkelsá	Width:	★★	
GPS:	64°53'43.7" N 23°48'44.0" W	Scenery:	★★★ ½	
(deg dec)	64.895472, -23.812222	Access:	2WD	Easy

Description

Svöðufoss ('Svodin's Falls') is an impressive waterfall falling off a cliff into a columnar basalt lined basin carved into the mountainside. It is much more beautiful than its neighbour Kerlingarfoss, although the latter is often marked on maps while the former is not. It is all the more interesting because of the two sub-falls below it.

Directions

Take Route 574 (Útnesvegur) to the village of Rif, midway between Hellissandur and Ólafsvik. Svöðufoss is clearly visible from the main road. At Rif take the road marked Svöðufoss. It forks right onto a dirt road, then bends right round back to the left, seemingly back the way you came from, before turning sharp right again to cross a bridge over the Hólmkelsá. Follow the road past an abandoned farm and park on the left where there is a parking area and the stream Fosslækur comes close to the road. You will see Keringarfoss at the end of the road, and it is worth a visit.

You will need to do some hiking across fences and heath that can sometimes be boggy. From where you parked, cross the stream and fence, and hike along the south side of the fence crossing the field. Continue about 550 m until you reach the Hólmkelsá river and a good view of the falls. When the water is low enough you can cross the river for a better view of the main falls from the other side.

If you want to get closer to Svöðufoss itself, you can climb the slope, but it is easiest to start at Kerlingarfoss. Take the dirt road to the right that climbs up the mountainside. Before the road crosses a small brook, turn off the road and hike 300 m across the heath in a north-westerly direction until you get to the waterfall.

Svöðufoss and sub-falls on the Hólmkelsá. GPS: 64°53'45" N 23°48'42" W (64.89583, -23.81167)

Kirkjufellsfoss

Region:	Vesturland	Facing:	E		
Town:	Grundarfjörður	Tiers:	2		
Area:	Grundarfjörður	Height:	★ ★ ★	9+8 m	
River:	Kirkjufellsá	Width:	★ ★ ★	17 m	
GPS:	64°55'34.5" N 23°18'43.7" W	Scenery:	★ ★ ★		
(deg dec)	64.926250, -23.312139	Access:	2WD	Easy	

Description

Kirkjufellsfoss ('Church Mountain Falls') is named after the mountain, Kirkjufell, that dominates the skyline to the north. It is the most photographed waterfall in the Snæfellsnes peninsula owing to its accessibility, two lovely tiers and the picturesque mountains on either side. There is a bridge over the river at the top of the falls.

Directions

Kirkjufellsfoss is along Route 574 (Útnesvegur), about 2.5 km west of the centre of the town of Grundarfjörður. There is a signposted car park where there is a small lagoon and where the road crosses the Kirkjufellsá. There is also a turnoff, east of the lagoon, onto a road that leads up to the bridge above the falls. From the bottom parking area, it is about 250 m along a well-marked trail to the top of the falls.

You should walk up over the bridge and round down the other side of the river, since the views from each side are quite different and equally pleasing. The view from the east bank takes in Kirkjufell in the distance.

Kirkjufellsfoss, a view of both tiers. GPS: 64°55'35" N 23°18'38" W (64.92639, -23.31056)

Fossárfoss (Selvallafoss)

Region:	Vesturland	Facing:	N-NW	
Town:	Grundarfjörður	Tiers:	4	
Area:	Hellgafellssveit	Height:	★★★	
River:	Fossá	Width:	★★	
GPS:	64°56'30.2" N 22°54'28.0" W	Scenery:	★★★ ½	
(deg dec)	64.941726, -22.907786	Access:	2WD	Easy

Description

Many people stop at the parking area to admire the view of the valley, then get back in their cars little realizing what they are missing a few hundred metres below them. Fossárfoss is a charming waterfall, not enormous, but easily making up for its lack of size in the beauty of its multiple tiers and wonderful, lush (in summer), steep twisting gorge. The name, which approximates to 'Waterfall On Waterfall-River' or 'Waterfall River Falls', is hardly inspirational, although the waterfall is also called 'Selvallafoss', stemming from Lake Selvallavatn below it. The four tiers fall about 24 m in total. The first tier is about 11 m high and overhangs a ledge, so you can scramble across the slopes and walk behind it.

Directions

From the south, drive up Route 54 (Snæfellsnesvegur) then north on Route 56 (Vatnaleið) towards Stykkisholmur. Pass Lake Baulárvallavatn and continue until you see a large parking area on the left, immediately after where the road crosses over the Fossá. If you are coming from the north, Grundarfjörður or Stykkisholmur, drive south on Route 56 past Lake Selvallavatn, until you see the large parking area on the right.

Walk across the rocky heath until you reach a good view of the waterfall (about 150 metres). There is no real trail but you should try to follow some of the more established paths. Continue further down the hillside, which can be quite steep, for views of all four tiers.

Fossárfoss is a charming four-tiered waterfall in a lovely gorge. You can walk behind the overhanging drop. GPS: 64°56'31" N 22°54'29" W (64.94194, -22.90806)

Þingmannaá Foss

Region:	Vestfirðir		Facing:	W	
Town:	Patreksfjörður		Tiers:	3	
Area:	Þingmannadalur, Vatnsfjördur		Height:	★ ★ ★ ★	
River:	Þingmannaá		Width:	★ ★	
GPS:	65°35'02.4" N 23°06'41.1" W		Scenery:	★ ★ ★ ★	
(deg dec)	65.584008, -23.111416		Access:	2WD	Easy

Description

Þingmannaá Foss ('Lawmaker Falls') is a little known but wonderful waterfall that should not be missed. The disjoined spelling is deliberate — there doesn't seem to be any other form of the name, such as 'Þingmannaáfoss' or 'Þingmannaáfossar'. It has an overall height of 32 to 35 m, with three tiers being about 14, 6 and 12 m high. You can walk behind one of the main chutes. The canyon itself is very interesting, originating from a volcanic eruption far beneath the surface. The location is so picturesque it was used in two films, *Útlaginn* ('The Outlaw') and *Nonni & Manni*.

Directions

Take Route 60 (Vestfjarðarvegur) to the Westfjords, and wind your way towards the town of Flókalundur in Vatnsfjörður. As the road comes to the end of the fjord it crosses the river Þingmannaá. You will see a parking area for a trailhead marked Lambagilseyrar that leads up the river towards the falls. It is a beautiful walk and only about 1 km to the top of the falls.

From the top of the falls you can continue on the Lambagilseyrar trail, marked with red flags, towards Lambagil canyon, then along the shore of Lake Vatnsdalsvatn and back to the parking by the main road. The entire loop of 7 km will take you about 2½ hours.

The three tiers of Þingmannaá Foss. GPS: 65°35'3" N 23°6'47" W (65.58417, -23.11306)

Dynjandi

Region:	Vestfirðir	Facing:	NW	
Town:	Bíldudalur	Tiers:	5	
Area:	Dynjandisvogur	Height:	★ ★ ★ ★	
River:	Dynjandisá	Width:	★ ★ ★ ★ ★	
GPS:	65°43'57.8" N 23°11'55.7" W	Scenery:	★ ★ ★ ★ ★	
(deg dec)	65.732707, -23.198818	Access:	2WD	Easy

Description

Dynjandi is one of Iceland's most magnificent waterfalls and therefore on many tourists' lists of must-see sights. It is however well away from the Route 1 circuit, so you must have already decided that you want to take the time to explore the Westfjords. Along with Dynjandi, you get seven sub-falls. Although Dynhandi is often referred to as the entire group of waterfalls, it is really the topmost one. There are six sub-falls as you climb along the main trail, up about 85 m in altitude, to Dynjandi itself; and there is one more, Kálfeyrarfoss, off to the side, accessible from the other side of the river.

In order of position going up the river, the sub-falls are:

- Bæjarfoss or Sjófoss ('Farm Falls', 5 m)
- Hundafoss ('Dog Falls', 2 m)
- Kálfeyrarfoss ('Calf Ear Falls', 5 m)
- Hrísvaðsfoss ('Trembling Ford Falls', 6 m)
- Göngumannafoss or Göngufoss ('Traveller's Falls', 8 m)
- Strompgljúfrafoss ('Chimney Canyon Falls', 20 m)
- Hæstajallafoss ('Talking Horse Falls', 8 m)

Dynjandi ('Thunderous Falls') is also known as Fjallfoss ('Mountain Falls'), Dynjandifoss or Dynjandafoss. It is one of Iceland's most spectacular waterfalls, although it does not owe its reputation to the volume of water that flows over it or its power. It is Dynjandi's tremendous size, a combination of both height and width, along with the step-like tiers of lacy, streaming water, that makes it such an awe-inspiring sight. The dimensions are not accurately documented, but the height is generally quoted as being around 100 m, with a width going from 30 m at the top to between 60 and 70 m at the base. There are five main discernible tiers, although these are in turn divided into many minor ledges. It is the combination of tiers and ledges that break up the waterflow into the fanning, lacelike veil that makes Dynjandi so marvellous.

Directions

It is straightforward to get to Dynjandi, but quite a long drive from just about anywhere. From the south, take the very long Route 60 (Vestfjarðavegur) northwards past Brjánslækur and over the mountains. As you descend back down towards the sea, you should spot Dynjandi on your left. There is a signposted turnoff towards a large managed car park with toilets, tourist information and camping facilities, just after the bridge over the river Dynjandisá.

From the car park, there is a trail that passes by the series of falls (except Kálfeyrarfoss), but it becomes quite rocky as you approach Dynjandi. The individual falls are helpfully signposted along the way. Although the final approach to Dynjandi is the steepest, it is nevertheless still very easy. The trail zigzags a little for about 200 m and arrives at the right-hand side of the pool below the waterfall. You can cross directly in front, and if you don't mind the spray you can approach very close to the waterfall. It takes about thirty minutes to climb up the winding path to Dynjandi but if you want to take in as many views as possible allow two hours for the full return trip.

Most people rush to see the famous Dynjandi and its six named sub-falls, paying little attention to the small cascade to the north of the main flow, where the river bifurcates around a small island. Kálfeyrarfoss is not accessible from the trail going up to Dynjandi, so you should see it first or last, starting from the north-east side of the bridge over the river. There is no trail.

Strompgljúfrafoss, Hæstajallafoss and Dynjandi. For an idea of scale, note the two people at the top of Strompgljúfrafoss. GPS: 65°44'3" N 23°12'16" W (65.73417, -23.20444)

Kolufoss (Kolufossar)

Region:	Norðurland vestra	Facing:	N	
Town:	Hvammstangi	Tiers:	1	
Area:	Víðidalur	Height:	★★★	
River:	Víðidalsá	Width:	★★★★	
GPS:	65°19'54.8" N 20°34'11.1" W	Scenery:	★★★★	
(deg dec)	65.331879, -20.569761	Access:	2WD	Easy

Description

Kolufossar is a series of waterfalls in Kolugljúfur canyon, which is about 1 km long and 40 to 50 m deep. From the rim, you have magnificent views of the rock walls, river and waterfalls below. The river Víðidalsá starts broadly on the upper plateau to form the 40 m wide main waterfall, usually just called Kolufoss, which falls into the tight canyon. Below Kolufoss the river is constrained by the canyon walls to a width of about 10 m.

You can easily view Kolufoss from the bridge and walk along the river to get closer to it. If you follow the canyon rim north, you will see Neðri-Kolufoss ('Lower Kola Falls'), a lovely tall waterfall squeezed by the gorge. You can also walk under the bridge and into the canyon.

Kolufossar derives its name from the ogress or troll called Kola, who according to legend created the canyon. There are even two places said to still exist from the time Kola lived there. In one spot is her bed, Kolurúm, and in another is her cauldron, in which she used to cook salmon from the river. The legend goes on to say that Kola and her treasure are buried in the nearby hill, which is protected by a spell.

On the way to Kolufoss, take the time to see Kerafossar. It is an enchanting maze of cascades with four drops in two tiers, including a very picturesque fish ladder. You could sit on the rocks above the river for hours and soak in the swirling beauty of it.

Directions

If coming from the west, take Route 1, heading east from Hvammstangi and turn south onto Route 715 (Víðidalsvegur). Drive about 4 km to where Route 715 doubles back on itself and take the dirt road that continues south.

If coming from the east, take Route 1, heading west from Blönduós and turn south onto Route 715 (Víðidalsvegur). Drive about 9 km to where Route 715 doubles back on itself and take the dirt road that continues south.

In both the above cases, continue along the dirt road for about 1.5 km, to the bridge that crosses the canyon and river. Park by the bridge.

For a detour to Kerafossar: when you are turn onto Route 715 drive about 1 km and cross the river Fitjá. Turn left onto the dirt road and go past the turnoff to a small waterfall called Kerhólsfoss. Go a further 400 m or so, following the road as it bends first to the right then to the left, until you reach a parking area near the river. It is about 100 m and an easy clamber over the rocks to the falls.

Kolufoss funnelling into Kolugljúfur canyon. As seen from the bridge. GPS: 65°19'57" N 20°34'13" W (65.33250, -20.57028)

Neðri-Kolufoss is squeezed by the canyon walls. Kolufoss can be seen in the distance. GPS: 65°19'60" N 20°34'17" W (65.33333, -20.57139)

Forsæludalur Waterfalls

Region:	Norðurland vestra			
Town:	Blönduós			
Area:	Forsæludalur	Access:	2WD	Easy to Strenuous

Description

Somewhere along Route 1 and almost due south of Blönduós is the junction with Route 722 (Vatnsdalsvegur) that leads to the valley of Forsæludalur. This valley is blessed with a lovely, deep and colourful canyon through which runs the river Vatnsdalsá. A string of waterfalls drop from 360 m above sea level to 80 m, over a distance of about 9 km. Starting at diminuitive Stekkjarfoss, you can view at least ten significant falls from a trail along the canyon ridge all the way to Skinandi, an impressive 20 m high waterfall. Although far less well-known than the Skógá trail in the south of Iceland, this northern counterpart, the Forsæludalur trail, is almost as rewarding. Unlike the Skógá trail, you are unlikely to meet more than a few fellow hikers, if any. This is partly due to the location, far removed from the more popular areas off Route 1, and perhaps because it is more difficult at times, despite the smaller gain in elevation, since there is no defined hiking trail and some initial sections are quite steep and taxing. Allowing for rough heath, confusing paths, and sometimes strong winds, as well as time to stop and take in the sights, you need to allow 5 to 7 hours for the full return trip.

At the trailhead there is an information panel kindly erected by the farmer with a map of the Forsæludalur trail.

The following sub-sections summarise the most noteworthy falls along the trail.

- Stekkjarfoss
- Dalfoss
- Friðmundaráfoss
- Skessufoss
- Landsendafoss
- Bergbúl
- Kerafoss
- Freyðandi
- Rjúkandi
- Skinandi

Directions

From the west, take Route 1 towards Blönduós. Approximately 17 km before the town turn onto Route 722 (Vatnsdalsvegur). Drive for 22.6 km and bear left off Route 722 on the road to Forsæludalur, staying to the east of the river. Drive all the way to Forsæludalur farm at the end, a total distance of 27.8 km. Park by the entrance to the farm, near the information panel for the Forsæludalur trail. (Do not drive onto the farm property.) The trailhead starts at the panel and heads down to the river.

Stekkjarfoss

River:	Vatnsdalsá	Tiers:	2	
Facing:	NW	Height:	★	
GPS:	65°17'53.4" N 20°05'35.7" W	Width:	★ ★	
(deg dec)	65.298163, -20.093262	Scenery:	★ ★	

Description

Stekkjarfoss is quite small but the apparent volume of water going over it is deceptive. The average flow of the river Vatnsdalsá in summertime is 8.5 m³/sec. There is a fish ladder to one side.

Directions

Start at the information panel with the map of the Forsæludalur trail and waterfalls. Stekkjarfoss is a short easy walk of about 1 km along a well-marked path. You will pass through two gates on the way.

Stekkjarfoss with fish ladder. GPS: 65°17'54" N 20°5'33" W (65.29833, -20.09250)

Dalfoss (Dalsfoss)

River:	Vatnsdalsá	Tiers:	1	
Facing:	NW	Height:	★★	
GPS:	65°17'20.2" N 20°04'31.3" W	Width:	★★★	
(deg dec)	65.288939, -20.075364	Scenery:	★★★ ½	

Description

Dalfoss is a picturesque block-shaped waterfall, divided part of the way along the top by a large rock. It is about 12 m high by 15 m wide. The canyon is particularly splendid in this area with mottled brown and green layers of rock gouged perpendicularly at regular intervals along its walls. You will be able to see that while it may be possible to hike along the river edge from Stekkjarfoss when the water level is very low, it is practically impossible at other times because of the steep canyon walls.

Directions

Dalfoss is about a 45-minute walk from the trailhead and 2 km from Stekkjarfoss. After Stekkjarfoss, when the trail seems to bend towards the river (for anglers), head up the steep slope until you get to the canyon ridge and a fence. At this point you have two choices: you can either climb the fence and follow the ridge around, which involves detouring around several side gullies; or you can follow the fence until you come to a farm track heading south-east. The latter is the easiest route but, since it is away from the canyon, you will need to know when to head back to the river. After about 1.25 km, when the track turns north-east, hike 400 m south-west across the heath to the canyon rim to where you can overlook Dalfoss.

Dalfoss set against the splendid canyon walls. GPS: 65°17'24" N 20°4'31" W (65.29000, -20.07528)

Friðmundaráfoss

River:	Friðmundará	Tiers:	1
Facing:	W	Height:	★★★
GPS:	65°17'19.2" N 20°03'20.9" W	Width:	★
(deg dec)	65.288660, -20.055800	Scenery:	★★★

Description

Friðmundaráfoss pours into the gorgeous canyon of Illiskurður that merges into Forsæludalur. The stream Friðmundará squeezes through a tight channel between the canyon walls before plunging over 20 m down into an amphitheatre lined with red and green-tinged rock walls. The Friðmundará then runs into the Vatnsdalsá.

Directions

From Dalfoss follow the canyon ridge for about 500 m up to and along that of Illiskurður.

Friðmundaráfoss plunges into Illiskurður, a side canyon off Forsæludalur. GPS: 65°17'20" N 20°3'59" W (65.28889, -20.06639)

Skessufoss

River:	Vatnsdalsá	Tiers:	2
Facing:	NW	Height:	★ ★ ★
GPS:	65°16'51.9" N 20°03'56.2" W	Width:	★ ★
(deg dec)	65.281094, -20.065605	Scenery:	★ ★ ★

Description

Skussufoss ('Ogress Falls') is a two-tiered waterfall, with the first and second tiers separated by 40 m. Together, they have a total height of around 20 m. The lower tier is the most interesting, as in the middle of the river there is a jumble of rocks which splits the falls into two channels at low water levels. The waterfall is tightly constrained by the surrounding canyon walls, which are similar to those at Dalfoss, but more barren and picturesque.

Directions

From Friðmundaráfoss, follow the ridge upwards until it meets a fence line. Follow this for a while and head down to the stream where there is a big boulder lying in and across the Friðmundará, forming a bridge. This boulder even has a name, Hlaupið, derived from an Old Norse word for 'leap' or 'jump'. Cross the stream and follow an indistinct, rough and very steep trail up the mountainside to the ridge. Once you have passed this section of the trail, the rest is easier going. There should be a marked, if sometimes obscure, path at the top. Follow it until you see Skussufoss. Along the way you will pass Flúðin, which are insignificant rapids, but nevertheless shown on the Forsæludalur trail map. Skussufoss is about 5 km walking distance from the trailhead.

Skessufoss is surrounded by layered canyon walls. GPS: 65°17'8" N 20°3'33" W (65.28556, -20.05917)

Landsendafoss

River:	Vatnsdalsá		Tiers:	1
Facing:	NW		Height:	★★★
GPS:	65°16'35.9" N 20°03'26.7" W		Width:	★★
(deg dec)	65.276632, -20.057408		Scenery:	★★★★

Description

Landsendafoss is a stately, block-shaped waterfall, almost 20 m square. The canyon walls on either side display an astonishing range of shades and colours, including red, green and golden brown. From your vantage point above the Vatnsdalsá, you can also see some unnamed falls in the distance, not far upriver from Landsendafoss.

Directions

Landsendafoss is about 600 m along the ridge from Skussufoss. Hiking can become a little confusing as the heath becomes rough and the marked trail disappears from sight. There is a plethora of sheep paths but these can lead you off in the wrong direction or into aimless zigzags. But if you stay close to the canyon rim you cannot go wrong, even if at times that requires winding your way round several side gullies.

Stately Landsendafoss within its multi-coloured canyon. GPS: 65°16'39" N 20°3'23" W (65.27750, -20.05639)

Bergbúl

River:	Vatnsdalsá	Tiers:	1	
Facing:	NE	Height:	★★	
GPS:	65°16'24.2" N 20°03'17.2" W	Width:	★	
(deg dec)	65.273401, -20.054768	Scenery:	★★★ ½	

Description

Bergbúl plunges about 10 m out of a tight turn in the river and drops into a pool within a steep-sided bowl. It is completely different from preceding waterfalls and a delightful sight. Although the height is modest, the sheer volume of the constrained plume of water causes a cloud of spray to billow up as the chute hits the pool below.

Directions

Bergbúl is about 400 m upriver from Landsendafoss.

Bergbúl makes a delightful picture as it plunges into a steep-sided bowl in the canyon. GPS: 65°16'29" N 20°3'11" W (65.27472, -20.05306)

Kerafoss (Kerárfoss)

River:	Vatnsdalsá	Tiers:	Multiple
Facing:	NW	Height:	★★★
GPS:	65°16'10.4" N 20°02'50.3" W	Width:	★★★★
(deg dec)	65.269550, -20.047311	Scenery:	★★★★

Description

Kerafoss is a big change compared to the previous waterfalls along the Vatnsdalsá. It is about 15 m high and multi-tiered, with the first step set a bit back from the rest. The main part of the falls is a sliding cascade fanning out slightly as it drops over a series of ledges. You could easily sit and watch the churning, frothing waters for quite some time. You can climb down to the river bank for a close-up view from below the falls.

Directions

Kerafoss is about 500 m upriver from Bergbúl.

Kerafoss is multi-tiered and fans out as a sliding cascade. GPS: 65°16'13" N 20°2'51" W (65.27028, -20.04750)

Freyðandi

River:	Vatnsdalsá		Tiers:	1
Facing:	NW		Height:	★ ★ ★
GPS:	65°15'44.1" N 20°01'40.2" W		Width:	★ ★ ★ ★
(deg dec)	65.262249, -20.027830		Scenery:	★ ★ ★ ★

Description

Freyðandi dramatically succeeds in being different from its predecessors. The deep canyon has now flattened out into a broad shallow valley. The river is also relatively broad and shallow here. The waterfall forms a wide, convex arc as it falls some 20 m into a deep cut formed by the river below it. Surrounding boulders add interest to an already beautiful vista. Watch out for clouds of spray near the falls.

Directions

Freyðandi is about 1.25 km upriver from Kerafoss.

Freyðandi forms a beautiful, convex arc and lots of spray as it drops into the gorge. GPS: 65°15'45" N 20°1'41" W (65.26250, -20.02806)

Rjúkandi (Rjúkandifoss)

River:	Vatnsdalsá		Tiers:	1
Facing:	NW		Height:	★★★
GPS:	65°15'24.9" N 20°01'10.9" W		Width:	★★★
(deg dec)	65.256922, -20.019682		Scenery:	★★★ ½

Description

Like Freyðandi, Rjúkandi ('Smoking Falls') stems from within a broad shallow valley. Here, the Vatnsdalsá is joined by another mountain stream just before it drops about 15 m into a wide basin. Like Kerafoss, Rjúkandi spreads out as it descends, to almost twice its topmost width.

Directions

Rjúkandi is about 750 m upriver from Freyðandi.

Rjúkandi fans out to almost twice its topmost width. GPS: 65°15'28" N 20°1'9" W (65.25778, -20.01917)

Skinandi (Skinandifoss)

River:	Vatnsdalsá	Tiers:	1	
Facing:	NW	Height:	★ ★ ★	
GPS:	65°15'14.0" N 20°00'42.9" W	Width:	★ ★ ★ ★	
(deg dec)	65.253891, -20.011928	Scenery:	★ ★ ★ ★	

Description

Maybe it's a case of keeping the best for last, although there is strong competition from some of the other waterfalls in the Forsæludalur valley. Skinandi is worth the slog to get there. It is a magnificent waterfall, 20 m high and twice as wide. Although the valley here is broad and shallow, the waterfall has a power and aura that gives it majesty even without the surrounding scenery. You will, however, usually have to contend with a lot of spray. If you have not yet had quite enough of waterfalls, you can also hike 150 m further upriver to a small, unnamed waterfall.

Directions

Skinandi is about 500 m upriver from Rjúkandi. You will have to climb over a fence in order to get close to the falls. The total walking distance from the trailhead is about 9 km.

Skinandi is a magnificent sight, even through the spray. GPS: 65°15'18" N 20°0'48" W (65.25500, -20.01333)

Reykjafoss

Region:	Norðurland vestra		Facing:	E	
Town:	Varmahlið		Tiers:	3	
Area:	Skagafjordur		Height:	★ ★ ★	
River:	Svartá		Width:	★ ★ ★ ★	
GPS:	65°29'41.0" N 19°22'58.6" W		Scenery:	★ ★ ★ ★	
(deg dec)	65.494715, -19.382947		Access:	2WD	Easy

Description

Reykjafoss is a fascinating, fan-shaped waterfall of three major tiers and many picturesque submerged rocky ledges. The falls face east, then the river turns sharply north. Above the waterfall the river is known as Svartá, it becomes the Huseyjarkvisl below the falls.

Directions

Reykjafoss is about 7 km from Route 1. From the west and the direction of Varmahlið, take Route 752 (Skagafjarðarvegur) and turn onto Route 753 (Vindheimavegur) to Vindheimar. Cross a bridge over the river and at the sign of a horse's head turn down the road that leads to Vindheimamelar farm. The name, meaning 'Smoking Falls', probably comes from the spray thrown up at the base. If you are coming from the east and the direction of Akureyri, it is shorter to take Route 753 directly until you come to the road that leads to Vindheimamelar farm.

Drive past the stables to a very large parking area for the horseracing track. There are two buildings on it. Go past these and turn left and continue to the end. Park by the double gate, go through the one on the right, and head towards the river for 600 m.

Reykjafoss fans out eastwards over three tiers, then the river turns sharply north. For an idea of scale, note the horse and hut in the distance. GPS: 65°29'43" N 19°22'54" W (65.49528, -19.38167)

Goðafoss

Region:	Norðurland eystra		Facing:	NE	
Town:	Akureyri		Tiers:	1	
Area:	Bárðardalur		Height:	★★★	9-17 m
River:	Skjálfandafljót		Width:	★★★★★★	135 m
GPS:	65°40'58.4" N 17°33'00.2" W		Scenery:	★★★★★	
(deg dec)	65.68289, -17.55006		Access:	2WD	Drive-up

Description

Goðafoss is one of the most well-known waterfalls in Iceland. It is a magnificent waterfall despite its modest height. Its beauty comes from its very broad horseshoe shape with two major sections and several minor ones. The colours of the water change a lot depending on the weather conditions, varying from muddy brown to sapphire blue.

From either side of the river you can hardly fail to miss Geitafoss, located downstream of Goðafoss and before the footbridge.

Goðafoss is closely connected with one of the most important events in Icelandic history, the conversion to Christianity from paganism or 'the old custom' in the year 1000. At that time, Iceland's legislative assembly, the Alþing, was debating which religion the Icelanders should practice. Þorgeir Þorkelsson, the Law Speaker of the Icelandic parliament lived on a farm, Ljósavatn, near the waterfall. As Law Speaker, he was faced with the task of settling the growing disputes between the Christians and those who still worshipped the old Nordic gods. After Þorgeir, himself a pagan priest, had spent a day and a night in silent meditation under a fur blanket he decided that Iceland should be a Christian country, although individuals could still practice paganism in private. Having made that decision, he thought that he should become a Christian too, so when he returned home, he threw his statues of the Norse gods into the waterfall to symbolise his conversion. As a result, the waterfall was thereafter called Goðafoss ('Waterfall of the Gods').

Geitafoss ('Goat Falls') is located downriver of Goðafoss, before the footbridge crossing the Skjálfandafljót. It can be viewed from both sides of the river and from in front, on the south side of the footbridge. It is quite a sight as all the turbulent water coming from Goðafoss is forced into the relatively tight channel.

Directions

Goðafoss is located just off Route 1, almost midway between Akureyri and Myvatn. It is about 43 km from Akureyri and 39 km from Myvatn, at the junction of Route 1 and Route 844 (Bárðardalsvegur Eystri). The parking area is signposted.

You can get a good view the falls after a very short walk from the main car park on the north side of the river, but you can best appreciate Goðafoss by walking up and down the trails and over the rocks on both sides to take in many varying views. There is also a parking area on the south side of the river.

Perhaps the best recommendation is to start at the northern parking area. Follow a path downstream along the gorge and cross the footbridge near the highway to get to the opposite side of the river. Follow the path as far as you can to reach a point overlooking Goðafoss. There you will get a different perspective and possibly even better view. The total distance is about a kilometre.

Goðafoss, viewed from the north-west side. GPS: 65°41'1" N 17°32'58" W (65.68361, -17.54944)

Goðafoss, viewed from the south-east side. GPS: 65°40'59" N 17°32'55" W (65.68306, -17.54861)

Aldeyjarfoss

Region:	Norðurland eystra		Facing:	NW	
Town:	Akureyri		Tiers:	1	
Area:	Bárðardalur		Height:	★ ★ ★	20 m
River:	Skjálfandafljót		Width:	★ ★	
GPS:	65°21'59.3" N 17°20'13.2" W		Scenery:	★ ★ ★ ★ ★	
(deg dec)	65.36647, -17.33700		Access:	4WD/SUV/2WD	Easy

Description

Aldeyjarfoss is one of Iceland's most scenic and most photographed waterfalls. Many Icelanders consider it their favourite. One of its most interesting features is the contrast between the orange and black basalt columns, and the white and blue waters of the falls with the churning cauldron below it. You can reach Aldeyjarfoss from both sides of the river. The views from each side are equally magnificent.

Directions

To reach the north side of Aldeyjarfoss: From Goðafoss take Route 844 (Bárðardalsvegur Eystri), then after about 22 km where it turns west over a large bridge, continue ahead on Route 843 (Lundarbrekkuvegur). After about 12 km you will see a succession of three signposts for Aldeyjarfoss. The last sign says it is 2.4 km to the waterfall. This section is rough and suitable only for 4WD vehicles or high ground clearance SUVs, so if you have a 2WD car you will have to walk. Park at the end of the track where the sign says walking is obligatory from that point.

Walk down the disused 4WD track to a dead end and take the trail down to a stream. Cross over the wooden footbridge and take the footpath to the left. Follow the stream for a short distance and keep a careful lookout for a fork. Follow the white markers going uphill to a good viewpoint overlooking the waterfall. It is about a 25-minute walk in all. (Note that if you miss the fork and continue to follow the stream, the trail will become very tortuous and quite difficult — even going through a tight cave — and you will end up past Aldeyjarfoss and closer to Ingvararfoss.) From Aldeyjarfoss, it is a 10-minute walk to Ingvararfoss and involves circumnavigating parts of the canyon (see the next entry).

To reach the south side of Aldeyjarfoss: From Goðafoss take Route 844 (Bárðardalsvegur Eystri), then after about 22 km go west over a long bridge. Turn left onto Route 842 (Bárðardalsvegur Vestri). (Note that it is also possible to take Route 842 directly from the west side of Goðafoss.) Continue on Route 842 until it becomes F26 (Sprengisandsleið). At this point, you should have a 4WD vehicle but the road as far as Aldeyjarfoss is quite good and usually passable in an SUV or even 2WD vehicle (although at your own risk). The waterfall is signposted and there is a good parking area with toilet facilities.

It is a 5-minute walk from the parking area, on a good path, to where you can overlook the waterfall. It is another 5 minutes to Ingvararfoss, which is signposted.

To get to the south side from the north side, or vice versa, you need to drive roughly 36 km in all, passing over the Skjálfandafljót via the bridge that links Routes 844 and 842.

Aldeyjarfoss, viewed from the north side of the canyon in the spring. GPS: 65°22'0" N 17°20'30" W (65.36667, -17.34167)

A view from the south side, looking upriver. GPS: 65°21'58" N 17°20'18" W (65.36611, -17.33833)

Ingvararfoss

Region:	Norðurland eystra	Facing:	W
Town:	Akureyri	Tiers:	1
Area:	Bárðardalur	Height:	★ ★
River:	Skjálfandafljót	Width:	★ ★ ★ ½
GPS:	65°21'57.9" N 17°19'41.9" W	Scenery:	★ ★ ★ ½
(deg dec)	65.366082, -17.328291	Access:	4WD/SUV/2WD Easy

Description

Ingvararfoss is a marvellous waterfall, well worth the extra effort after seeing Aldeyjarfoss. The height is very dependent on the water flow, being somewhere over 6 m. The span is in two sections, a wide main section of 20 to 25 m and a small one of about 3 m.

Directions

Follow the directions to Aldeyjarfoss. The waterfall is a 5-minute walk from Aldeyjarfoss on the south side along a good path. It will take you about 10 minutes on the north side, but there is no trail and it is not a straightforward scramble over the rocks from Aldeyjarfoss since you need to negotiate the canyon walls.

Ingvararfoss, viewed from the north side. GPS: 65°21'58" N 17°19'43" W (65.36611, -17.32861)

Hrafnabjargafoss

Region:	Norðurland eystra	Facing:	N	
Town:	Akureyri	Tiers:	1	
Area:	Bárðardalur	Height:	★★	
River:	Skjálfandafljót	Width:	★★★★★★	
GPS:	65°20'23.7" N 17°20'24.9" W	Scenery:	★★★★★	
(deg dec)	65.339925, -17.340242	Access:	4WD/SUV	Easy

Description

Amid the charcoal-black sands and twisted lava looms the misty, grey waterfall, Hrafnabjargafoss. Somehow, even the name, 'Raven's Rock Falls' conjures a sense of mystery. Hrafnabjargafoss is about 3 km upriver from Aldeyjarfoss and Ingvararfoss. Not just a sight to behold, but many sights, because you need to see the falls from many different places and angles. Such is the vast breadth of this majestic waterfall, it presents greatly different views over its four or five sections. Multitudes of separate cascades drop off a 200 m long ledge that crosses diagonally over the wide river. The most spectacular section is at the upper, U-shaped, southern end, but these falls deserve the time spent walking all along its length and over the rocks above it.

Directions

Follow the directions to the south side of Aldeyjarfoss. Pass the turnoff to Aldeyjarfoss and continue on F26 for about 2.9 km. Hrafnabjargafoss is signposted but the track to the waterfalls is almost non-existent. You will need to follow tyre marks that twist and turn for about 500 m to an area close to the falls that serves for parking.

Hrafnabjargafoss is a multitude of falls crossing the river diagonally. GPS: 65°20'24" N 17°20'30" W (65.34000, -17.34167)

Dettifoss

Region:	Norðurland eystra	Facing:	NW		
Town:	Reykjahlíð	Tiers:	1		
Area:	Jökulsárgljúfur	Height:	★ ★ ★ ★	45-50 m	
River:	Jökulsá á Fjöllum	Width:	★ ★ ★ ★ ★	100-150 m	
GPS:	65°48'52.3" N 16°23'03.9" W	Scenery:	★ ★ ★ ★ ★		
(deg dec)	65.814535, -16.384416	Access:	2WD	Easy	

Description

Dettifoss ('Tumble Falls') is reputed to be the most powerful waterfall in Europe with a mean summer volume of about 400 m³/s. It is also in a most dramatic setting, making this one of the three most visited waterfalls in Iceland. Its height is between 45 and 50 m and its width is usually quoted as being 100 m but may be considerably more than that, with some sources estimating it as over 150 m. It is easy to get to, with ample parking, as demonstrated by the large number of tourist buses that regularly make this a prime destination. While the best views are probably to be had on the east side, the west bank affords views that more directly face the falls. Depending on the weather, a considerable amount of spray can reach the viewing areas, especially on the west bank, so be prepared.

Directions

Dettifoss can be reached from the north and south, for both east and west sides. The easiest is from the south and east.

East side:

From the south: From Myvatn, take Route 1 to Route 864 (Hólsfjallavegur) heading north. It is about 31 km to the signposted turnoff, and a short 3 km drive takes you to a managed parking area with toilet facilities.

From the north: Starting from the ranger station at Ásbyrgi, take route 85 (Norðausturvegur) east for about 2.5 km, then Route 864 (Hólsfjallavegur) going south 26 km to the signposted turnoff for Dettifoss. It is about 2 km south of the road to Hafragilsfoss. As above, a short drive then takes you to a managed parking area.

It is a good 10- to 20-minute walk along a marked trail of about 500 m, down some steps and across a rather rocky path to the canyon rim and various sightseeing points. There is a railed viewpoint that on good days provides a fabulous view of the waterfall from a distance, and takes in the canyon walls on either side. On bad days you will get drenched by spray and see absolutely nothing. A favourite spot is right at the top of the falls looking along the line of the drop, but it is a slight scramble across the rocks to get there, and best made with good shoes.

If you go back along the trail towards the parking area, you will see that it branches at one point, with a signpost indicating the path to Selfoss (see the next entry). If you return to Route 864 and head north for about 2 km, you will get to the turnoff for Hafragilsfoss (see the previous entry).

West side:

From the south: From Myvatn, take Route 1 to Route 862 (Dettisfossvegur) heading north. After about 20 km, follow directions to Dettifoss taking the dirt road off Route 862. A short drive takes you to a very large parking area with toilet facilities, where an easy walk will take you to a view of the canyon and waterfall.

From the north: From Route 85 (Norðausturvegur), west of the ranger station at Ásbyrgi, take Route 862 (Dettisfossvegur) going 29.4 km south to the turnoff to Dettifoss. As above, a short drive then takes you to a very large parking area.

There is short easy walk of about 700 m to the upper rim of the canyon above Dettifoss. The view at this point is nowhere near as spectacular as from the east side but on a good day you can get closer by taking the slippery path down to the lower rim. When you see the dot-like sightseers on the east side of the river, you will appreciate the size of Dettifoss and the considerable distance between you and the ridge opposite. On a bad day, the walk down can be quite treacherous and immersed in spray. The path may even be closed at certain times of the year.

If you go back along the trail towards the parking area, you will see that it branches at one point with a signpost indicating the path to Selfoss (see the next entry). If you go back towards Route 862, there is a turnoff to Hafragilsfoss (see the previous entry).

The east bank of the Jökulsá á Fjöllum. You can spot two people on top of the rock overlooking Dettifoss. GPS: 65°48'58.7" N 16°23'04.9" W (65.816313, -16.384684)

Sitting at the top of Dettifoss. GPS: 65°48'55" N 16°23'2" W (65.81528, -16.38389)

A view from the upper rim of the west bank. GPS: 65°48'50" N 16°23'12" W (65.81389, -16.38667)

Selfoss

Region:	Norðurland eystra	Facing:	W-NE	
Town:	Reykjahlíð	Tiers:	1	
Area:	Jökulsárgljúfur	Height:	★ ★ ½	11-13 m
River:	Jökulsá á Fjöllum	Width:	★ ★ ★ ★ ★ ★	
GPS:	65°48'18.0" N 16°23'11.9" W	Scenery:	★ ★ ★ ★ ½	
(deg dec)	65.805007, -16.386634	Access:	2WD	Easy

Description

Considering the number of people who visit Dettifoss, it is surprising how few make the additional effort to see Selfoss, a truly magnificent waterfall. It is a wonderful, majestic sight, a combination of a narrow horseshoe and a long ridge of overflowing black bedrock. At this point, the Jökulsá á Fjöllum is very wide and deceptively peaceful as it makes its way down to Dettifoss. At Selfoss the river basin changes from a broad, featureless volcanic plain to a stark ravine carved into columnar basalt. Here the river has gouged a narrow notch in the basalt formations to form a long, tightly-pinched, horseshoe-shaped canyon. While the tip of the horseshoe seems to funnel the vast majority of the river, the remaining water pours down from shallow pools all along the long length of the western ridge, and it is this section that really gives Selfoss its majesty. This enormous expanse, of the order of 400 m in length, makes Selfoss possibly the widest waterfall in Iceland. You can see Selfoss from both the east and west banks, and in both cases the starting point is Dettifoss. (For an explanation of the falls' name, see the entry for Selfoss in Búlandsdalur, Austurland.)

Directions

East side:

Follow the directions for Dettifoss. From the parking area, it is an initial 10- to 20-minute walk along a marked trail of about 500 m, down some steps and across a rather rocky path to the canyon rim. Along the path, close to Dettifoss, there is a wooden sign pointing out the trail heading upriver to Selfoss. You have to negotiate about 1.2 km of quite rocky and sometimes muddy and indistinct trail to get to the lower portion of the falls, with about another 400 m to get to the top. It is well worth the extra 15- to 30-minute walk and rock hopping, the time depending on your nimbleness. The best views are usually a little downriver from the very tip and, depending on the weather, you might not be able to approach the horseshoe without being drenched in spray and your vision very obscured.

West side:

Follow the directions for Dettifoss. From the parking area, there is short easy walk of about 300 m to where the path forks, with a signpost indicating the way to Selfoss. You can also take a loop trail from Dettifoss to Selfoss and back to the parking area. It is about a 5-minute easy walk to get to the lower part of the waterfall. Getting to the top however is another matter. Much of the water flows over the western bedrock and in the process forms large pools of water that prevent access to the rim. Therefore, while it is easy to get some good views at the lower end of Selfoss on this side, it is almost impossible to get anywhere near the top without a lot of wading.

Selfoss, from halfway along the east bank. GPS: 65°48'22.0" N 16°23'12.6" W (65.806121, -16.386840)

Selfoss, seen from the west bank. GPS: 65°48'29" N 16°23'23" W (65.80806, -16.38972)

Hafragilsfoss

Region:	Norðurland eystra	Facing:	NW	
Town:	Reykjahlíð	Tiers:	1	
Area:	Jökulsárgljúfur	Height:	★ ★ ★ ½	27 m
River:	Jökulsá á Fjöllum	Width:	★ ★ ★ ★ ★	85 m
GPS:	65°49'56.3" N 16°24'01.6" W	Scenery:	★ ★ ★ ½	
(deg dec)	65.832299, -16.400434	Access:	2WD	Drive-up

Description

A little downriver from Dettifoss, Hafragilsfoss is the second largest waterfall in the Jökulsá á Fjöllum and the second most powerful waterfall in Europe. The river drops 27 m off a straight ledge of volcanic bedrock into a beautiful chasm with cliff walls facing the chute.

The most scenic view of Hafragilsfoss (and it is a spectacular view) is from the east side and high above the river. In any case, it is extremely difficult to get any closer on that side. There is a magnificent vista of the river and Hafragil canyon, and it is also the side for the best views of Dettifoss and Selfoss. If you want a close-up view of Hafragilsfoss, you need to go to the west side and hike down to the canyon rim above the falls.

Directions

Hafragilsfoss can be approached from the north and south, for both east and west sides. The easiest is from the south and east.

East side:

From the south: Follow the directions for Dettifoss. From there, the turnoff for Hafragilsfoss is about 2 km north of that for Dettifoss, and is signposted. A short drive takes you to a managed parking area with a good view from high above the canyon and waterfall.

From the north: Starting from the ranger station at Ásbyrgi, take route 85 (Norðausturvegur) east for about 2.5 km, then Route 864 (Hólsfjallavegur) going south 24 km to the signposted turnoff for the waterfall. As above, a short drive then takes you to a small parking area.

Although you have an excellent view from the car park, it is a shame not to take the trail to the north and walk for about 5 minutes along the ridge for a few different perspectives and a good view north of the Jökulsá á Fjöllum and canyon.

West side:

From the south: Follow the directions for Dettifoss, taking the dirt road off Route 862 as if going to Dettifoss. A short distance down the road there is a signposted left turn to the left for Hafragilsfoss. A short drive then takes you to a small parking area, where an easy walk will take you to a view of the canyon and waterfall.

From the north: From Route 85 (Norðausturvegur), west of the ranger station at Ásbyrgi, take Route 862 (Dettisfossvegur) going 29.4 km south to the turnoff to Dettifoss and Hafragilsfoss. As above, a short distance down the road there is a signposted left turn to the left for Hafragilsfoss and a short drive then takes you to a small parking area.

From the parking area, it is about a 200 m easy walk to a view of the waterfall, but it is nevertheless a little high and the view is somewhat obscured by the canyon rim. There is an information panel showing two hiking trails for a closer and better view of the waterfall. It is about a 1 or 1½ hour hike depending on if you do the full loop. Parts of the trail can be quite precipitous, slippery or boggy, but perseverance will get you to the rim of the promontory, right in front of Hafragilsfoss.

The Jökulsá á Fjöllum and Hafragilsfoss, viewed from the east side parking area. GPS: 65°50'10" N 16°24'2" W (65.83611, -16.40056)

Hafragilsfoss, seen from a viewpoint a couple of minutes down the trail. You should be just able to make out the path down from the west rim. GPS: 65°50'10" N 16°24'9" W (65.83611, -16.40250)

Æðarfossar

Region:	Norðurland eystra	Facing:	W	
Town:	Husavik	Tiers:	3	
Area:	Aðaldalur	Height:	★★	
River:	Laxá	Width:	★★★★★★	
GPS:	65°58'57.4" N 17°24'54.7" W	Scenery:	★★★ ½	
(deg dec)	65.982599, -17.415193	Access:	2WD	Drive-up

Description

Æðarfossar ('Eider Falls') is a very photogenic waterfall, easy to get to and worth the trip. Although it is only about 9 m high, with two very low tiers and a prominent third, it spans the river Laxá ('Salmon River') in three well-defined sections with an overall width of around 140 m. It makes a most scenic picture with the large outcrops of rock, and the turbulent river channelled between them and descending to the sea.

Directions

Take Route 85 (Norðausturvegur) heading to Husavik. After junction 85/87 go 500 m past the farm immediately on the left, then take a left turn onto a dirt road to another farm. At the T-junction turn right onto Laxamýrarvegur. Follow the road as it turns sharp left towards a third farm. Still on Laxamýrarvegur, veer right at the farm and go to the very end of the road. There is a small hut and a parking area, mostly used by anglers, that overlook the falls.

Not a good spot to fish, but a great one to admire the waterfall. You can see the people on the rock, a place only reachable by boat. GPS: 65°59'00" N 17°24'51" W (65.98333, -17.41417)

Sandárfoss

Region:	Norðurland eystra	Facing:	NE	
Town:	Þórshöfn	Tiers:	Multiple	
Area:	Þistilfjörður	Height:	★ ★	
River:	Sandá	Width:	★	
GPS:	66°08'38.5" N 15°40'05.0" W	Scenery:	★ ★ ★ ★	
(deg dec)	66.144030, -15.668049	Access:	2WD	Easy

Description

Sandárfoss ('Sandy River Falls') is a small but gorgeous waterfall. Set in a narrow gully, the turbulent river Sandá ('Sandy River') tumbles down multiple natural steps over a distance of about 100 m while water pours in from pools along the sides. It makes a splendid sight and is not to be missed.

Directions

Sandárfoss is south of Rauarhofn and west of Þórshöfn, off Route 85. Take Route 85 (Norðausturvegur) to Flaga farm. Take the dirt road that seems to be the farm entrance. Go round the farm and drive for 5.4 km, through one gate, right to the end, then park.

For much of the distance to the waterfall there is no obvious trail. Walk about 2 km, over sometimes very boggy heath, by following the river until you come to a fence. Cross over and continue for about 200 m beyond it until you reach the waterfall.

Sandárfoss tumbles down, and down, and down. GPS: 66°8'40" N 15°40'0" W (66.14444, -15.66667)

Gljúfursárfoss

Region:	Austurland	Facing:	E	
Town:	Vopnafjörður	Tiers:	1	
Area:	Vopnafjörður	Height:	★ ★ ★ ★ ★	
River:	Gljúfursá	Width:	★ ★	
GPS:	65°44'45.1" N 14°40'21.2" W	Scenery:	★ ★ ★ ★	
(deg dec)	65.745873, -14.672554	Access:	2WD	Easy

Description

Gljúfursárfoss ('Canyon River Falls') is a magnificent waterfall in an astounding, geologically varied, and mossy, bowl-shaped canyon. (Gljúfursárfoss should not to be confused with the Gljúfrafoss, also called Gljúfurárfoss, in the south, near the famous Seljalandsfoss). It is surprising how these falls are little-known outside of the local area considering their amazing beauty. The Gljúfursá originates on the almost 1 km high Vindfellsfjöll Mountain, and the canyon is just before the river flows into the Vopnafjörður fjord. It is a pity that Route 917 passes just above the waterfall and detracts a touch from its beauty, but it is easy to cut it out of photographs.

There is a lovely 2.2 km circular trail starting from Gljúfurárfoss going along Route 917 to Drangsnes canyon and then looping back. It is a beautiful canyon and coastline, with an ancient historical connection to the sagas, Njál's Saga begins at this location.

Directions

From Vopnafjörður, head south then take Route 917 (Hlíðarvegur) eastwards. Continue for about 9.3 km east of junction 917/919 to a parking area for the waterfall. From there, the viewpoint is only 100 m away.

Gljúfursárfoss is a stunning waterfall in a beautiful canyon. GPS: 65°44'49" N 14°40'28" W (65.74694, -14.67444)

Rjúkandi

Region:	Austurland		Facing:	SE	
Town:	Egilsstadir		Tiers:	2	
Area:	Jokuldalur		Height:	★ ★ ★ ★ ★	33+60 m
River:	Ysta-Rjúkandi		Width:	★ ★ ½	
GPS:	65°20'04.1" N 15°04'52.5" W		Scenery:	★ ★ ★ ★	
(deg dec)	65.334474, -15.081235		Access:	2WD	Easy

Description

Rjúkandi (meaning 'Smoking', and surprisingly named neither 'Rjúkandifoss' nor 'Ysta-Rjúkandifoss') is a magnificent waterfall in the spring and early summer, although it dries up considerably later on. The Ysta-Rjúkandi is one of many rivers that flows down the steep mountainside into the valley of Jökuldalur and into the Jökulsá a Brú river. Rjúkandi is rather unusual as it drops first 33 m onto flattish bedrock, then splits and drops the remaining 60 m, bouncing off a small ledge on the way down before recombining at the bottom. The sister waterfall, Fremsta-Rjúkandi Fossar is next door, and Garðafoss is worth a quick stop, just 3.7 km east of Rjúkandi.

Directions

Rjúkandi is located off Route 1 near the village of Skjöldólfsstadir and is about 4.1 km east of the junction 1/923. The river is signposted. There is parking at the Rjúkandi picnic area 200 m to the west. You can easily see Rjúkandi from the road but there is access through a gate and it is an easy hike to get a closer and far more interesting look.

Rjúkandi is a magnificent waterfall with a unique form. GPS: 65°19'57" N 15°4'39" W (65.33250, -15.07750)

Gufufoss

Region:	Austurland		Facing:	W	
Town:	Egilsstaðir		Tiers:	2	
Area:	Fljótsdalur		Height:	★★★	6+13 m
River:	Miðhúsaá		Width:	★★	5-8 m
GPS:	65°16'01.1" N 14°19'39.0" W		Scenery:	★★★	
(deg dec)	65.266964, -14.327507		Access:	2WD	Easy

Description

Gufufoss is on the river Miðhúsaá as it winds its way down the mountainside of Fjardarheiði. (It should not be confused with another Gufufoss not far from here, also along Route 93, but on the river Fjarðará.) The falls are about halfway up the trail to the better-known Fardagafoss (see the next entry).

At the parking area, there is a useful information panel about the trail and history behind the two falls. Gufufoss can be roughly translated as 'Steam Falls', so called because of the constant spray that drifts high into the air above it where the falls drop into the gorge and strike against the rock walls as the river makes a sharp right turn. Gufufoss is two-tiered, about 19 m high, and 5 to 8 m wide depending on the water flow.

Directions

From Egilsstaðir take Route 93 (Seyðisfjarðarvegur) towards Seydisfjordur. Continue 2 km past junction 93/94 to where there is a signposted parking area. Take the trail to Fardagafoss. It is an easy 5- to 10-minute walk to Gufufoss.

The river Miðhúsaá makes a sharp turn after Gufufoss. GPS: 65°16'4" N 14°19'42" W (65.26778, -14.32833)

Fardagafoss

Region:	Austurland		Facing:	W	
Town:	Egilsstaðir		Tiers:	1	
Area:	Fljótsdalur		Height:	★ ★ ★ ★	28 m
River:	Miðhúsaá		Width:	★ ★	8 m
GPS:	65°16'08.2" N 14°18'49.5" W		Scenery:	★ ★ ★	
(deg dec)	65.268932, -14.313736		Access:	2WD	Easy

Description

Fardagafoss, located further up the trail from the lesser-known Gufufoss, plunges 28 m through a constriction in the cliff walls lining the river. It is the plume and the shapes and colours of the fractured rocks all around that provide its beauty. There is a useful information panel about the trail and history behind the falls at the parking area.

The name Fardagafoss comes from the term Fardagar, the four-day period in early summer when Icelanders were allowed to move their residence to tend farms, although why the waterfall took the name is unclear. There is a cave behind the waterfall that is accessible thanks to an overhang protecting the entrance, and an unnamed small waterfall a little below Fardagafoss.

Directions

Follow the directions for Gufufoss. From there, the trail continues upwards and can be quite steep at times. Getting to the cave is not easy but a chain is fastened in the cliff to help you climb down to it. It should take you from 10 to 20 minutes to get to Fardagafoss from Gufufoss, and less than an hour for the full round trip from and to the car park.

There is a cave behind Fardagafoss. GPS: 65°16'8" N 14°18'55" W (65.26889, -14.31528)

Seyðisfjörður Waterfalls

Region: Austurland
Town: Seyðisfjörður
Area: Seyðisfjörður   Access: 2WD   Easy to Vigorous

Description

The river Fjarðará starts high up above the town of Seyðisfjörður, fed by the melting snows covering the highland moor of Fjarðarheiði and the mountaintops, and flows down through the town into the fjord, also called Seyðisfjörður. A series of waterfalls drop about 320 m from an intermediate plateau and is closely followed by the road into the town. A very pleasant 5 km trail leads from a historical power station at the bottom to Múlafoss, the waterfall at the top.

According to a signpost at the top of the trail, there are 25 waterfalls in total, but the definition of a uniquely identifiable waterfall is unclear. Many of the cascades along the river are no bigger than rapids, and most falls have no name, or the names have been lost with time. For this reason, in this guide, the numbering allocated to the waterfalls along the trail is purely subjective and a best estimate.

The trail and river almost follow the road to the town of Seyðisfjörður but the only way to see the marvels along this very beautiful stretch is to walk, since there are few stopping places along the road and in many places the waterfalls are not visible from it anyway. As an alternative to attempting to hike from the power station, which is a little difficult without going back to the road, visit the Fjarðarselsvirkjun waterfall first, then drive to Gufufoss, which is close to the road and where it is easy to park. You can, of course, also park at Múlafoss and hike down. Assuming that you parked your car at Gufufoss, then the hike down to Neðri-Úðafoss and up to Múlafoss should take you about 1½ hours.

The list below and following sub-sections summarise the most noteworthy falls along the Fjarðará trail.

- Fjarðarselsvirkjun waterfall
- Neðri-Úðafoss
- Efri-Úðafoss
- Gufufoss
- Múlafoss (the lower)
- Systrafossar
- Skutarfoss
- Ragnarfoss
- Stöppufossar
- Múlafoss (the upper)

A further waterfall, Búðarafoss (also called Búðarárfoss or Búðareyrarfoss), is a prominent feature of Seyðisfjörður, very visible on the east side of the town. Melting snow from the Strandartindur mountain feeds into the Búðará, which then drops over a cliff and ends up in Seyðisfjörður fjord. It is easy to reach the falls' base; and if you are adventurous, you can hike up the slope to the top and even go from there to another unnamed waterfall of about the same height as Búðarafoss, about 200 m further upstream.

Directions

For the parking area at Gufufoss: From the Hotel Aldan at the entrance to Seyðisfjörður town, drive up Route 93 (Seyðisfjarðavegur) for about 3.4 km. It will be difficult to miss the waterfall as it is so close to the road and obvious. There is a parking area at a bend in the road. Leave the car there and walk back along the river bank as far as you wish before returning to the road and back to Gufufoss. From there you should follow the river up the rest of the way to Múlafoss. You can then walk or get a lift back down the road to your car.

For the parking at Múlafoss: From Egilsstaðir take Route 93 (Seyðisfjarðarvegur) towards Seydisfjordur. The parking area for Múlafoss is difficult to miss. It is at the first major bend in the road as it comes downhill towards Seyðisfjörður. It is about 5.9 km from the entrance to Seyðisfjörður town at Hotel Aldan.

Búðarafoss is just a short walk away from the main road in Seyðisfjörður. GPS: 65°15'48" N 13°59'41" W (65.26333, -13.99472)

Fjarðarselsvirkjun Falls

River:	Fjarðará		Tiers:	1
Facing:	NE		Height:	★★
GPS:	65°14'35.7" N 14°01'54.8" W		Width:	★
(deg dec)	65.243248, -14.0319		Scenery:	★★

Description

The Fjarðarselsvirkjun hydroelectric plant is Iceland's oldest operational power plant, put into service in October 18th 1913. The plant marked a turning point in the history of Icelandic electrification. It was the first power plant in Iceland to generate alternating current as well as being the power station of the first municipal electric utility. The first high-voltage cable in Iceland was also laid from this station. You can visit a small museum upon request.

The waterfall behind the power plant is pretty but unnamed. It is the first of the series of waterfalls that make up the Fjarðará trail.

Directions

From the entrance to Seyðisfjörður town, at Hotel Aldan, drive up Route 93 (Seyðisfjarðavegur) for about 1.7 km to the turn-off for the power station where there is a large a parking area.

The Fjarðarselsvirkjun hydroelectric plant and waterfall behind it. GPS: 65°14'43" N 14°1'48" W (65.24528, -14.03000)

Neðri-Úðafoss

River:	Fjarðará	Tiers:	1
Facing:	E	Height:	★
GPS:	65°14'26.0" N 14°02'46.9" W	Width:	★
(deg dec)	65.240566, -14.046357	Scenery:	★ ★ ½

Description

Neðri-Úðafoss ('Lower Misty Falls') would hardly be noteworthy were it not for the overall charm of the setting, with Efri-Úðafoss in the background. Joining the Fjarðará at this point is a small stream with its own small cascade alongside the other, so the width of Neðri-Úðafoss is debateable. There was once a signpost here bearing the name of the falls but it has long since succumbed to the ravages of the weather.

Neðri-Úðafoss is the fourth in a series of some 25 waterfalls — depending on how they are defined and identified — that make up the 5 km Fjarðará waterfall trail leading from the power station at the bottom to Múlafoss at the top.

Directions

If you are hiking from the power station, follow the directions for the Fjarðarselsvirkjun waterfall and hike up the road and river bank from there. If you are parking at Gufufoss, follow the directions for Gufufoss and hike down the trail to Neðri-Úðafoss.

Neðri-Úðafoss and joining stream in the foreground with Efri-Úðafoss in the background. GPS: 65°14'26" N 14°2'44" W (65.24056, -14.04556)

Efri-Úðafoss

River:	Fjarðará	Tiers:	1
Facing:	E	Height:	★★★
GPS:	65°14'24.5" N 14°02'58.4" W	Width:	★★
(deg dec)	65.240129, -14.049567	Scenery:	★★★ ½

Description

Efri-Úðafoss ('Upper Misty Falls') is a very attractive two-barrelled waterfall that drops over a rock ledge into a small cauldron-shaped gorge and circular pool. The name possibly comes from the spray or mist generated at the base of the falls. At the time of writing, there is still a weathered wooden signpost here bearing the name of the falls but it may not last much longer.

Efri-Úðafoss is the fifth in a series of some 25 waterfalls that make up the 5 km Fjarðará waterfall trail leading from the power station at the bottom to Múlafoss at the top.

Directions

If you are hiking from the power station, follow the directions for Neðri-Úðafoss and hike up the river bank from there. If you are parking at Gufufoss, follow the directions for Gufufoss and hike down the trail to Efri-Úðafoss.

Efri-Úðafoss is a lovely, two-barrelled waterfall. GPS: 65°14'26" N 14°2'52" W (65.24056, -14.04778)

Gufufoss

River:	Fjarðará		Tiers:	1	
Facing:	E		Height:	★★★ ½	27 m
GPS:	65°14'23.9" N 14°03'27.2" W		Width:	★★	
(deg dec)	65.239972, -14.05757		Scenery:	★★★ ½	

Description

Gufufoss is a striking waterfall that drops over a sharp rock ledge into a bowl-shaped gorge and shallow circular pool. Gufufoss has the largest single drop of all the waterfalls along the Fjarðará. As a result of its height and the rocks below, there is a considerable amount of spray generated at the base of the falls and this gives Gufufoss its name, which roughly means 'Steam Falls'. It should not be confused with another Gufufoss not far from here, also along Route 93, but on the river Miðhúsaá.

Gufufoss is the sixth in a series of some 25 waterfalls that make up the 5 km Fjarðará waterfall trail leading from the power station at the bottom to Múlafoss at the top.

Directions

From the entrance to Seyðisfjörður town, at Hotel Aldan, drive up Route 93 (Seyðisfjarðavegur) for about 3.4 km. You will have a hard time missing the waterfall, as it is so close to the road and obvious. There is a parking area.

Gufufoss generates a considerable amount of 'steam'. GPS: 65°14'26" N 14°3'18" W (65.24056, -14.05500)

Múlafoss

River:	Fjarðará	Tiers:	2	
Facing:	NE	Height:	★ ★ ½	12+2 m
GPS:	65°13'50.9" N 14°04'41.8" W	Width:	★ ★	
(deg dec)	65.230795, -14.078286	Scenery:	★ ★ ★ ½	

Description

Múlafoss is similar to Efri-Úðafoss. It is an attractive, two-barrelled waterfall that drops over a rock ledge into a small cauldron-shaped gorge and circular pool. It is confusing that there are two waterfalls having the same name on the same river, but this Múlafoss is not the well-known Múlafoss at the top of the trail. There is a battered wooden signpost here bearing the name of the falls but it is deteriorating.

Múlafoss is the seventh in a series of some 25 waterfalls that make up the 5 km Fjarðará waterfall trail leading from the power station at the bottom to the bigger Múlafoss at the top.

Directions

Follow the directions for Gufufoss. Múlafoss is about 400 m west of Gufufoss.

Múlafoss (the lower and less well-known Múlafoss) falls in two plumes into a picturesque basin. GPS: 65°14'26" N 14°3'47" W (65.24056, -14.06306)

Systrafossar

River:	Fjarðará	Tiers:	1	
Facing:	NE	Height:	★★	
GPS:	65°14'20.9" N 14°04'10.2" W	Width:	★★	
(deg dec)	65.239141, -14.069496	Scenery:	★★★ ½	

Description

Systrafossar ('Sisters Falls') is similar to the two lower falls, Efri-Úðafoss and Múlafoss. It is an attractive, two-barrelled waterfall that drops over a rock ledge into a small cauldron-shaped gorge and circular pool. Although the name implies several falls, it is not known why this particular waterfall is so named, other than it might refer to the the two plumes. There was once a signpost here bearing the name of the falls but it has long since rotted away in the merciless weather.

Systrafossar is the eighth in a series of some 25 waterfalls that make up the 5 km Fjarðará waterfall trail leading from the power station at the bottom to Múlafoss at the top.

Directions

Follow the directions for Gufufoss. Systrafossar is about 150 m west of Múlafoss.

The distinctive two channels of Systrafossar. GPS: 65°14'23" N 14°4'6" W (65.23972, -14.06833)

Skutafoss & Ragnarfoss

River:	Fjarðará	Tiers:	1
Facing:	NW	Height:	★★
GPS:	65°14'10.4" N 14°04'34.5" W	Width:	★★★
(deg dec)	65.23623, -14.076259	Scenery:	★★★ ½

Description

Skutafoss and Ragnarfoss are the twelfth and fourteenth waterfalls in the series of some 25 waterfalls that make up the 5 km Fjarðará waterfall trail. They are part of a cluster of four main falls, in parallel groups of two, on a section of the river that forks around a small island then recombines. Together they make a very attractive sight. There is a rotting signpost here bearing the name of Skutafoss, and another stating that the name Ragnarfoss came from the occasion when a man — presumably called Ragnar — drove his car into the waterfall! Both wooden signs have deteriorated to the point of being almost unreadable and cannot last much longer. The data and ratings are for Ragnarfoss, the largest of the four falls.

Directions

Follow the directions for Gufufoss. The group of waterfalls is about 900 m south-west of Systrafossar.

Four falls. Skutafoss is on the right and Ragnarfoss is in the background on the same side. GPS: 65°14'11" N 14°4'35" W (65.23639, -14.07639)

Stöppufossar

River:	Fjarðará	Tiers:	2
Facing:	E	Height:	★★
GPS:	65°13'53.1" N 14°04'36.0" W	Width:	★★★
(deg dec)	65.231416, -14.076652	Scenery:	★★★ ½

Description

Stöppufossar comprises the twenty-first and twenty-second waterfall in the series of some 25 waterfalls that make up the 5 km Fjarðará waterfall trail. It is just below Múlafoss, and above a section of the Fjarðará, called Múlabraeður, that includes several small waterfalls. The plural ending of the name, Stöppufossar, implies several falls, so possibly the small cascade immediately below the large one is regarded as part of the same waterfall. This guide assumes it is. There was once a signpost here but it has disintegrated over the years.

Directions

Follow the directions for Gufufoss. Stöppufossar is about 600 m south-west of Ragnarfoss.

Stöppufossar is ostensibly the larger waterfall in the middle of the picture, but probably includes the lower cascade. The lower tier of Múlafoss can be seen in the distance. GPS: 65°13'54" N 14°4'34" W (65.23167, -14.07611)

Múlafoss (Mulafoss, Múlifoss)

River:	Fjarðará	Tiers:	3	
Facing:	E	Height:	★★★★	
GPS:	65°13'50.8" N 14°04'41.6" W	Width:	★★★	
(deg dec)	65.230786, -14.078236	Scenery:	★★★★	

Description

Múlafoss (sometimes spelled Mulafoss, without the accented 'u') is the collective name given to the twenty-third, twenty-fourth and twenty-fifth waterfalls in the series of some 25 waterfalls that make up the 5 km Fjarðará waterfall trail. Múlafoss, or Múlifoss after the river Múli that joins the Fjarðará at this point, can refer to any or all of the upper three big drops on the river. While there is a signpost on the rock above the falls mentioning the 25 waterfalls descending to Seyðisfjörður, there is no actual mention of Múlafoss.

The first part of the falls is a big drop of about 10 m into a very narrow slot. This then opens up and drops about 8 m into a pool that then cascades nearly 20 m over broken rocks to a broad slab forming the riverbed. To get the best view of the falls you need to cross the footbridge over the Fjarðará and work your way down on the other side of the river. Note that this Múlafoss is different from the one of the same name further downstream. This Múlafoss is about 400 m walking distance from Stöppufossar.

If you are hiking the Fjarðará waterfall trail and you parked your car at Gufufoss then the walk down to Neðri-Úðafoss and up to Múlafoss should take you about 1½ hours.

Directions

From Egilsstaðir take Route 93 (Seyðisfjarðarvegur) towards Seydisfjordur. The parking area for Múlafoss is difficult to miss. It is at the first major bend in the road as it comes downhill towards Seyðisfjörður, and is about 5.9 km from Hotel Aldan at the entrance to the town of Seyðisfjörður.

The second and third tiers of Múlafoss as viewed from the south side of the river. A few cars and people are visible at the top of the picture, giving scale to the waterfall. GPS: 65°13'51" N 14°4'37" W (65.23083, -14.07694)

Klifbrekkufossar

Region:	Austurland	Facing:	NE	
Town:	Egilsstaðir	Tiers:	7	
Area:	Fjarðardalur	Height:	★★★★★	90 m
River:	Fjarðará í Mjóafirði	Width:	★★	
GPS:	65°10'46.2" N 14°04'53.6" W	Scenery:	★★★	
(deg dec)	65.179495, -14.081555	Access:	2WD	Drive-up

Description

The Klifbrekkufossar waterfalls are close to the end of the Mjóifjörður fjord, not far from Egilsstaðir. The waterfalls are on the river Fjarðará í Mjóafirði (to distinguish it from another Fjarðará near Seyðisfjörður). They cascade down the mountainside in a series of zigzag steps within grassy slopes and scraggy cliffs. The river originates from a small drainage basin above the falls that accumulates water from a multitude of runoff streams and a few small mountain lakes.

Klifbrekkufossar can be translated approximately as 'Hillside Waterfalls', which is a very apt name. The total height of the falls is about 90 m, falling in seven major steps, although some sources say that there are as many as nine.

Directions

From Egilsstadir, drive south on Route 92 (Norðfjarðarvegur) for 8.5 km then turn onto Route 953 (Mjóafjarðarvegur) towards Mjóifjörður. Drive about 16.5 km over many switchbacks until you see a sign on the right for Klifbrekkufossar. You can park by a picnic table. From there it is easy to view the waterfalls, but a short walk back up the road and along a trail can take you close to the lowest of them, a double-barrelled waterfall of about 6 m in height. There is no trail to the top of Klifbrekkufossar but if you are well equipped, you can scramble up the slopes to get there.

The lower four tiers of Klifbrekkufossar. GPS: 65°10'50" N 14°4'43" W (65.18056, -14.07861)

Litlanesfoss (Stuðlabergsfoss)

Region:	Austurland	Facing:	SW-SE	
Town:	Hallormsstaður	Tiers:	2	
Area:	Fljótsdalur	Height:	★ ★ ★ ★	
River:	Hengifossá	Width:	★ ½	
GPS:	65°05'02.0" N 14°53'02.5" W	Scenery:	★ ★ ★ ★	
(deg dec)	65.083903, -14.884025	Access:	2WD	Easy

Description

Litlanesfoss ('Little Falls') is arguably more beautiful than its bigger and more famous brother, Hengifoss, a little further up the river (see the next entry). Litlanesfoss drops in two tiers, the first falling about 6 m into a small pool and the second about 35 m turning 90° as it does so. The fascination of Litlanesfoss is the stark geological terrain all around, with large and spectacular outcrops of fractured columnar basalt encasing the waterfall on both sides.

Directions

Follow the directions for Hengifoss.

From the parking area, pass through the gate and take the stepped trail to Hengifoss. It is about 1 km to the first viewpoint of Litlanesfoss, and along the way, about halfway up the trail, you will pass another waterfall, Jónsfoss, which is a little over 15 m high. If you want to explore further, there is also a trail leading down to the bottom of the gorge.

The two-tiered Litlanesfoss twists between spectacular columnar basalt outcrops. Hengifoss can be seen in the distance. GPS: 65°4'54" N 14°52'57" W (65.08167, -14.88250)

Hengifoss

Region:	Austurland	Facing:	S		
Town:	Hallormsstaður	Tiers:	1		
Area:	Fljótsdalur	Height:	★ ★ ★ ★ ★	118 m	
River:	Hengifossá	Width:	★ ★		
GPS:	65°05'02.0" N 14°53'02.5" W	Scenery:	★ ★ ★ ½		
(deg dec)	65.095398, -14.890414	Access:	2WD	Moderate	

Description

Hengifoss ('Hanging Falls') is one of Iceland's tallest waterfalls. It plunges off a high plateau and falls about 118 m into a massive, very broad amphitheatre. The cliff sides are geologically unique, being composed of thick, dark layers of volcanic bedrock that sandwich thin beds of bright red mud and ash between them.

Directions

From Egilsstadir, drive south on Route 931 (Upphéraðsvegur) and cross the long bridge over the river Lagarfljót and the start of Lake Lagarfljót. Then turn south onto Route 933 (Fljótsdalsvegur). There is a well-established parking lot with toilet facilities and an information panel immediately after the bridge over the river Hengifossá.

Pass the gate and take the stepped trail to Hengifoss. It is about a 500 m walk after Litlanesfoss on a pleasant trail to reach a good viewpoint, then it is about another 1 km to the end of the trail on a moderately steep, rough path that crosses a stream. From the parking area, it is about 2.5 km in total, and you should assume a good hour. Where the trail ends, the base of the waterfall is still hidden from view. You need to cross the river and scramble up the scree slopes to get closer.

Hengifoss falls 118 m into a massive amphitheatre. GPS: 65°5'12" N 14°53'4" W (65.08667, -14.88444)

Laugarfell Highland Waterfalls

Region:	Austurland
Town:	Hallormsstaður
Area:	Fljótsdalur	Access:	2WD	Easy to Strenuous

Region: Austurland
Town: Hallormsstaður
Area: Fljótsdalur   Access: 2WD   Easy to Strenuous

Description

The Laugarfell Highland Waterfalls are a group of four fabulous waterfalls clustered around the Laugarfell Highland Hostel (a wonderful, cosy and very welcoming retreat). The waterfalls can all be seen in one 9 km circular trail, beginning at the hostel, either starting or ending with Slæðufoss, and passing Stuðlafoss, Faxi and Kirkjufoss.

There is a story circulating in the hostel of one fit runner who completed the entire 7 km portion of the loop (Stuðlafoss, Faxi and Kirkjufoss) in an hour and a half, but if you intend to take your time to soak up the views and negotiate your way around the worst boggy areas, count on three to five hours, plus twenty to thirty minutes to see Slæðufoss.

Directions

From Egilsstadir, drive south on Route 931 (Upphéraðsvegur) and cross the long bridge over the river Lagarfljót as it flows into Lake Lagarfljót. Then turn south onto Route 933 (Fljótsdalsvegur) and then onto Route 910 (Austurleið/Laugarfellsvegur). Continue until you see a signpost indicating the Laugarfell Highland Hostel on your left. The turning is just before Route 910 bends sharply to the west. Park in the hostel parking area.

The geothermally heated Laugarfell Highland Hostel. GPS coordinates: 64°53'09.2" N 15°21'05.7" W (64.885886, -15.351589).

Slæðufoss

River:	Laugará	Tiers:	1	
Facing:	S	Height:	★★	
GPS:	64°53'12.6" N 15°22'01.9" W	Width:	★★★	
(deg dec)	64.886823, -15.367197	Scenery:	★★★	

Description

Slæðufoss ('Veil Falls') is 5 to 8 m high, depending on the river conditions, and around 20 m wide. The river Laugará comes down from the highland plateau and falls into a lovely pool at the base of multi-coloured cliffs before turning sharply east and continuing its path to join the Jökulsá í Fljótsdal, 3 km downriver.

Directions

Follow the directions for the Laugarfell Highland Waterfalls. From the hostel, walk back along the road to where a bridge crosses the river, then take the path that leads you to the south side of the waterfall. It is about 1 km in walking distance from the hostel.

Slæðufoss is a short walk from the Laugarfell Highland Hostel. GPS: 64°53'10" N 15°21'55" W (64.88611, -15.36528)

Stuðlafoss

River:	Laugará	Tiers:	3
Facing:	E	Height:	★★★★
GPS:	64°53'31.9" N 15°19'42.6" W	Width:	★★ ½
(deg dec)	64.892186, -15.328503	Scenery:	★★★ ½

Description

Stuðlafoss is a three-tiered waterfall with the second tier forming a sliding ramp to the third that drops in its turn onto a mass of boulders in the riverbed. The main chute falls about 14 m and is surrounded by magnificent cliffs of columnar basalt. The next two tiers drop about 2 m and 8 m respectively. In the summer months, when the water level is lower, the large rocks in the middle of the river split the third drop into two channels. Stuðlafoss is the first stop on a 7 km loop back to the hostel. You can add a there-and-back walk to Slæðufoss to make it a full 9 km for the four waterfalls.

Directions

Follow the directions for the Laugarfell Highland Waterfalls. From the hostel parking area, walk to the north-east corner of the grounds. You will see a signpost marking the start of the trail. Follow the yellow markers that are roughly parallel to the Laugará and you will reach Stuðlafoss after about 2 km.

Stuðlafoss is a three-tiered waterfall with a total height of about 24 m. GPS: 64°53'28" N 15°19'28" W (64.89111, -15.32444)

Faxi (Faxifoss, Laugarárfoss)

River:	Jökulsá í Fljótsdal	Tiers:	1	
Facing:	NE-E	Height:	★★★ ½	27 m
GPS:	64°53'29.1" N 15°19'07.1" W	Width:	★★★ ½	25 m
(deg dec)	64.891431, -15.318641	Scenery:	★★★★★	

Description

Faxi is an astounding waterfall at the confluence of the Laugará and the Jökulsá í Fljótsdal. It is a marvellous sight. It has two main sections, one being mainly due to the Jökulsá and one due to the Laugará (hence its alternative name of Laugarárfoss). What particularly makes this location wonderful is the many different viewpoints of the two rivers as they meet and the different perspectives of Faxi and the canyon below it.

Directions

Follow the directions for the Laugarfell Highland Waterfalls. From the hostel parking area, walk to Stuðlafoss. About 0.5 km further along the trail you will reach Faxi at the point where the two rivers merge. For a great view, cross the Laugará via the little footbridge and make your way along the hillside a little way. To continue the hike, you will need to cross back over the bridge and thence along the bank of the Jökulsá í Fljótsdal.

Faxi. You can just see the Laugará joining the Jökulsá í Fljótsdal from the right. GPS: 64°53'32" N 15°19'8" W (64.89222, -15.31889)

Kirkjufoss

River:	Jökulsá í Fljótsdal	Tiers:	2	
Facing:	NE-E	Height:	★ ★ ★ ★	35-40 m
GPS:	64°52'12.4" N 15°20'44.9" W	Width:	★ ★ ★ ★	
(deg dec)	64.870104, -15.345813	Scenery:	★ ★ ★ ★ ★	

Description

When you reach Kirkjufoss ('Church Falls'), after several kilometres along the Jökulsá í Fljótsdal canyon rim, the view takes your breath away. This is the highest waterfall on the river. There are two distinct sections, at 45° to one another and separated by a massive rock face. They plummet some 35 to 40 m into a large bowl carved out of the mountainside. There is also a very substantial second tier that flows out of the bowl, but is only visible from the east side of the canyon.

After admiring Kirkjufoss, head west to get back to the Laugarfell Highland Hostel. The return trip is not as pleasant as the outward since the ground can be very boggy as you venture up the slopes, and the yellow markers can be quite difficult to find and follow. It is about 2 km back to the hostel.

Directions

Follow the directions for the Laugarfell Highland Waterfalls. You can walk directly to Kirkjufoss from the hostel, a distance of about 2 km, following yellow markers across what can be very boggy ground. However if you are doing the full round trip of the Laugarfell Highland waterfalls then follow the directions below.

From Faxi follow the yellow markers along the canyon rim, across what can be very marshy ground, for 3 km to reach Kirkjufoss. The markers can become very widely separated and difficult to spot, but by sticking close to the canyon you cannot go wrong.

Awe-inspiring Kirkjufoss. On the left is the start of the outgoing second tier. GPS: 64°52'12" N 15°20'40" W (64.87000, -15.34444)

Strútsfoss

Region:	Austurland	Facing:	NW	
Town:	Hallormsstaður	Tiers:	2	
Area:	Suðurdalur	Height:	★ ★ ★ ★ ★ ★	
River:	Strútsá	Width:	★ ★	
GPS:	64°53'37.5" N 15°01'18.7" W	Scenery:	★ ★ ★ ½	
(deg dec)	64.893741, -15.021852	Access:	2WD	Vigorous

Description

One of Iceland's tallest and most impressive waterfalls, Strútsfoss, is located where the river Strútsá falls into the Villingadalur branch of the Suðurdalur valley, within the deep Strútsgil canyon. The waterfall plunges in two tiers into a huge layered amphitheatre that is almost hidden in a side valley of Suðurdalur. It is similar to Hengifoss both in form and in the bowl-shaped cliffs around it, with layered strata and interleaved reddish stripes. While less accessible than Hengifoss, Strútsfoss is perhaps more impressive, with the two tiers making up a total height of between 120 and 180 m (depending on the source of information), the first tier being about a fifth the height of the second.

Strútsfoss derives its name from the river Strútsá and Strútsgil canyon. 'Strúts' is similar in meaning to the English 'struts', having a connotation of straight, upright or stiff. This probably refers to one or more of the pyramidal rocks standing in the gorge.

Directions

From Egilsstadir, drive south on Route 931 (Upphéraðsvegur) Where it turns to cross the long bridge over the river Lagarfljót continue south on Route 933 (Fljótsdalsvegur), then at its end turn onto Route 935 (Suðurdalsvegur). Drive to the end of 935 to Sturluflöt farm. Before the entrance to the farm, there is a parking area on the right with an information panel.

Take the signposted trail on the east bank of the river Kelduá and follow it upstream. This by-passes the farm property. The trail crosses a stream and turns left to follow the river Fellsá behind the farm. You will come to an old road and a signpost that indicates the proper trail. You will start to see red markers. Pass a bridge spanning the river — do not cross it — and keep on the trail heading upwards. It is about 3.5 km and 1 hour to a cairn and the first full view of the waterfall. At this point the trail becomes indistinct and climbs steeply on a sometimes slippery slope. It is about another 15 minutes of more strenuous hiking, but still following the red markers, to reach a magnificent view of the falls and canyon. The round trip should take about 2½ hours.

It is quite difficult to reach the base of the waterfall. It involves descending into the gorge and crossing the river several times. For the more adventurous, there is a circular trail, indicated on the information panel, that climbs to the canyon rim above the waterfall, back down the other side of Strústgil canyon and across the footbridge.

Strútsfoss as it first comes into view in Strútsgil canyon. GPS: 64°54'11" N 15°2'28" W (64.90306, -15.04111)

A great view at the end of the trail along the canyon. GPS: 64°54'12" N 15°2'28" W (64.90333, -15.04111)

Sléttufoss

Region:	Austurland	Facing:	N	
Town:	Reyðarfjöður	Tiers:	3	
Area:	Áreyjdalur	Height:	★ ★ ★ ★	
River:	Sléttuá	Width:	★	
GPS:	65°00'51.2" N 14°15'18.9" W	Scenery:	★ ★ ★	
(deg dec)	65.014220, -14.255237	Access:	2WD	Easy

Description

Sléttufoss is a delightful waterfall in a very picturesque gorge. In fact, it is so picturesque that photographs of Sléttufoss can look like paintings, with daubs of vivid green and mottled brown splattered over the canvas. The name, Sléttufoss, is derived from that of the river, Sléttuá, which translates roughly to 'smooth' or 'flat' river. So 'Sléttufoss' can be understood as meaning 'Flat River Falls'. The waterfall is over 30 m high and drops over the cliff edge in three tiers, although they are more like bumps over small ledges.

Directions

From Egilsstadir, drive south on Route 92 (Norðfjarðarvegur) to Reyðarfjörður. Then, west of the town, take Route 96 (Suðurfjarðavegur) south for 1.1 km and turn onto F936 (Þórdalsheiðarvegur). Despite being classified as a 4WD road it is fine for regular 2WD vehicles at least as far as the waterfall. Park before the farm, also called Slettuá, which is only 250 m up the road.

Climb over the fence and head east to where a footbridge spans the river Sléttuá. Cross the bridge and walk up to the waterfall. It is only about 1 km but as there is no path and the ground is rough, it should take between 20 and 30 minutes.

Sléttufoss drops over 30 m into a delightful gorge. GPS: 65°0'59" N 14°15'12" W (65.01639, -14.25333)

Flögufoss

Region:	Austurland		Facing:	NE	
Town:	Breiðdalsvik		Tiers:	1	
Area:	Suðurdalur		Height:	★ ★ ★ ★ ★	60 m
River:	Flöguá (Flaga)		Width:	★	
GPS:	64°49'05.2" N 14°22'42.3" W		Scenery:	★ ★ ★ ½	
(deg dec)	64.818123, -14.378415		Access:	2WD	Easy

Description

At around 60 metres, Flögufoss is the highest waterfall near Breiddalsvik. The river Flöguá (also called Flaga) runs through the valley of Flögudalur (or Flagadalur) and into the larger Suðurdalur and then Breiðdalur. As it passes over the cliff-top, it flows through a natural arch that forms an eye at the top of the waterfall. The view of the valley with Flögufoss and two other falls above it in the distance, surrounded by moss-covered slopes and backed by a craggy skyline is magnificent. It is no less so when you get close, with the striated amphitheatre, rock arch at the top of the falls and turquoise pool at the base.

Just 9.3 km south on Route 966, you can take a look at the 70 m wide Beljandi.

Directions

From Breiðdalsvik, take Route 1 until you come to Route 966 (Suðurbyggðarvegur) going south-west. There is a signpost to Flögufoss at the intersection and it is about 2 km to the waterfall. Park near a gate on the north side of the road opposite the falls in the distance. Cross the road and follow a partial trail that fades out and reappears at various times. It is about 1 km and a 20- to 30-minute walk to get close to the waterfall.

The view of Flögufoss from a distance is very impressive. GPS: 64°49'17" N 14°22'25" W (64.82139, -14.37361)

Folaldafoss

Region:	Austurland	Facing:	N	
Town:	Djupivogur	Tiers:	1	
Area:	Berufjörður	Height:	★★★	16 m
River:	Berufjarðará	Width:	★	
GPS:	64°48'13.2" N 14°33'34.2" W	Scenery:	★★★	
(deg dec)	64.803662, -14.559514	Access:	2WD	Drive-up

Description

Route 939, commonly known as Öxi Pass, passes through Öxi, a sparsely vegetated moor between the Skriðdalur valley and Berufjarðarbotn. The road is a 19 km shortcut for Route 1 that knocks some 60 km off the driving distance from Höfn to Egilsstaðir. Although it can be dangerous in bad weather as it is a gravel road and quite steep in places with tight hairpins, it is usually fine for regular vehicles during the summer months. It is a very pretty route and has at least two noteworthy waterfalls, Folaldafoss and Hænubrekkufoss.

The river Berufjörður drains water and melting snow from the high mountains above it and from the many small lakes in the surrounding moors. It maintains a significant volume all year round, particularly since the valley can retain snow banks for much of that time. The river comes down the mountain in a south-east direction, then suddenly twists sharply north as it squeezes through two large blocks of rock. Folaldafoss ('Colt Falls') then falls straight down into an attractive pool in a large, partially hollowed-out grotto. The outflow then turns again, and resumes its general south-easterly descent to the sea. Although the waterfall faces north, the large cliffs to the west can cast shadows in the afternoon that affect the view, so Folaldafoss is best seen from the morning to midday, or late in the evening.

Directions

From Route 1 and the town of Berufjörður, take Route 939 (Axarvegur) for about 2.3 km. Folaldafoss is clearly visible from the road. There is a turnoff and an ample parking area with picnic tables. You can easily view the falls from there but you will need to scramble a little down the slopes to get closer and a better perspective.

If you are coming from the north, Folaldafoss is 2.3 km south of Hænubrekkufoss.

Folaldafoss falls into a basin within a large, partially hollowed-out grotto. GPS: 64°48'19" N 14°33'31" W (64.80528, -14.55861)

Hænubrekkufoss

Region:	Austurland	Facing:	SE	
Town:	Djupivogur	Tiers:	3	
Area:	Berufjörður	Height:	★ ★ ★ ★ ½	
River:	Berufjarðará	Width:	★ ★	
GPS:	64°48'31.9" N 14°36'41.2" W	Scenery:	★ ★ ★	
(deg dec)	64.808871, -14.611458	Access:	2WD	Easy

Description

Hænubrekkufoss has three distinct tiers. The overall height is between 50 and 55 m, with the lowest part being some 30 m. The latter can easily be reached but the upper two sections are hard to get to. There is a pleasant aquamarine-tinted pool at the base.

Directions

From the south, follow the directions for Folaldafoss. Hænubrekkufoss is about 2.5 km northwest of that waterfall. There are several small places to pull over, just up the hill after the apex of the curve, where the falls are most visible, but there is no clear and spacious parking area anywhere nearby. Perhaps the best place is at a very small spot just above where the road bends sharply and is closest to the waterfall, underneath the power lines that cross above the road.

You can easily view Hænubrekkufoss from the road, which is the best place to see all three tiers. However, you can only appreciate its full size by getting close. You can reach the waterfall in about 10 minutes by walking back to the big bend in the road, hopping over the guardrail and then hiking down the mossy slope. There is no trail, but the terrain is not very difficult.

If you are coming from the north, from the direction of Egilsstaðir, take Route 1 south to Route 939 (Axarvegur), also known as Öxi Pass, then continue for about 15 km. Hænubrekkufoss is visible from the road. As above, park near the power lines.

Hænubrekkufoss has three tiers. GPS: 64°48'38" N 14°36'8" W (64.81056, -14.60222)

Sveinstekksfoss (Fossárfoss)

Region:	Austurland	Facing:	SE	
Town:	Djupivogur	Tiers:	1	
Area:	Fossárdalur	Height:	★★★	
River:	Fossá	Width:	★★	
GPS:	64°45'10.0" N 14°29'06.8" W	Scenery:	★★★★	
(deg dec)	64.752774, -14.485227	Access:	2WD	Drive-up

Description

Sveinstekksfoss ('Pig Pen Waterfall') may not be stunningly high, but even at 'only' 15 m it is nevertheless a magnificent waterfall. The ferocity of the water as it collides with an enormous boulder halfway down and rebounds high into the air almost shakes you. There are some small sub-falls a few metres down, and larger ones where the river crashes round the gorge walls, although these are almost hidden from view.

Directions

From the town of Djúpivogur, take Route 1 in the direction of Egilsstaðir for 14.5 km to the bridge over the river Fossá, then turn left onto a dirt road leading to the Eyjólfsstaðir Hostel. The road climbs steeply, and after only 500 m loops tightly up and to the right. The waterfall is clearly visible from the road. Park immediately after the bend, in a spacious, flat parking area. It is only a few steps to a railed viewpoint at the apex of the bend. An even better view involves an easy scramble onto a rocky promontory above the river.

Of moderate height, but what a sight as Sveinstekksfoss crashes over the rocks. GPS: 64°45'12" N 14°28'55" W (64.75333, -14.48194)

Snædalsfoss

Region:	Austurland	Facing:	NE	
Town:	Djupivogur	Tiers:	2	
Area:	Snædalur	Height:	★ ★ ★ ★	
River:	Snædalsá	Width:	★	
GPS:	64°38'34.9" N 14°32'18.7" W	Scenery:	★ ★ ★	
(deg dec)	64.643021, -14.538532	Access:	2WD	Easy

Description

Snædalsfoss ('Snow Valley Falls') is a striking, two-tiered waterfall, somewhere around 37 m in height, set against dark, looming cliffs and a jagged skyline. Mossy banks below the cliffs slope down to a shallow pool. The stream then winds its way down into broad flats before joining the sea at Hamarsfjörður.

Directions

From the town of Djúpivogur, take Route 1 in the direction of Höfn for 10.5 km and cross the bridge over the river Hamarsá. You can see the falls from there. About 600 m further on, take the dirt road to a farm and Bragðavellir Cottages. If you have a 2WD vehicle, you should park there. If you have a 4WD vehicle or high clearance SUV, you can drive past the farm and further into the valley. Park where you feel is best.

As you pass the farm, you can make a short detour to see a beautiful old bridge on the right. Otherwise, from the farm stay on the left and hike or drive 1.25 km further into the valley. Snædalsfoss is on the left. You can walk to the base of the falls.

Snædalsfoss is a striking, two-tiered waterfall set against dark, looming cliffs and a jagged skyline. GPS: 64°38'39" N 14°32'8" W (64.64417, -14.53556)

Hangandifoss

Region:	Austurland	Facing:	SE	
Town:	Höfn	Tiers:	1	
Area:	Mulagljufur	Height:	★ ★ ★ ★ ★ ★	
River:	Fosslaekur	Width:	★ ★	
GPS:	63°59'24.8" N 16°28'03.4" W	Scenery:	★ ★ ★ ★ ½	
(deg dec)	63.990224, -16.467612	Access:	2WD	Moderate

Description

Hangandifoss ('Hanging Falls') is one of the tallest and least well-known waterfalls in Iceland. It stems from the Öræfajökull glacier, and is not far from the much-visited Jökulsárlón and Breiðárlón glacial lagoons. It is, however, not obviously accessible and barely documented. The waterfall occurs where the Fosslaekur stream falls into the river Mulaá in Mulagljufur canyon. The canyon is spectactular, a hidden gem, and one of the most beautiful in Iceland. Hangandifoss falls from a crack in the cliff walls and plummets a distance of around 120 m into a large grotto, hitting a slight ledge halfway down. It is amazing that this waterfall is not better-known.

Directions

From Höfn, take Route 1 west past Jökulsárlón and continue for 3.3 km after the sign for Fjallsárlón to an intersection with a dirt road. From the south, it is about 19.5 km east of the N1 service station at the southernmost point of Öræfi. Turn on to the dirt road (GPS: 63°59'19.2" N 16°23'41.9" W or 63.988665, -16.394966). The road is rough but should be passable for most 2WD vehicles if driven carefully. Drive for 2.2 km to the end, and park.

There is a half-hidden trail just left of the flood dike that soon becomes a good path with wooden markers. It is relentlessly upwards but not too steep. It is easy to get lost here, so be careful not to lose sight of the markers when the trail bends to the right and crosses over to the next ridge. You will not see any sign of the canyon or waterfall for a while until you suddenly come to the rim. It is about 2.2 km from the parking area to the viewpoint. In the distance on the left, you should also be able to spot Múlafoss. You can hike about 1 km further along the ridge to get a closer view.

Along the way and only about 100 m or so from the view above Hangandifoss, is another pretty and fairly large but unnamed waterfall. It is on the other side of the ridge and fed by a different stream.

Hangandifoss in Mulagljufur canyon, with Múlafoss in the distance. GPS: 63°59'21" N 16°27'48" W (63.98917, -16.46333)

Hangandifoss falls 120 m into a deep grotto. GPS: 63°59'21" N 16°27'48" W (63.98917, -16.46333)

Skaftafell Waterfalls

Region:	Austurland
Town:	Kirkjubæjarklaustur
Area:	Skaftafellsheiði

Access: 2WD Vigorous

Description

The Svartifoss trail is a very popular hike within the Skaftafell National Park. You start at the Skaftafell Visitor Centre and go in a loop, following the river to the renowned waterfall from which the trail takes its name, then return on the other side, passing through the enormous Skaftafell campsite. The total round-trip distance is 5.5 km and takes about 2 hours plus stops. The river, (actually not much more than a stream) is commonly called the Bærjargil although this really denotes the gorge through which it runs. The river's official name may be the Skaðá, but this is by no means clear.

(Note that although the Skaftafell National Park is often talked of as being in the south of Iceland, the Suðurland region, it is actually located at the westernmost edge of the Austurland region).

The wide and moderately steep trail passes four named waterfalls. In an anticlockwise direction, these are:

- Hundafoss
- Magnúsarfoss
- Svartifoss
- Þjófafoss

Two other significant waterfalls are nearby and just off the main trail. These are:

- Heygötufoss
- Austurheiðarfoss

Directions

Skaftafell National Park is located off Route 1. From the west, it is 66 km east of the roundabout in Kirkjubæjarklaustur, and from the east it is 54 km west of Jökulsárlón. Take the turnoff for Route 998 (Skaftafellsvegur) which is also signposted for Skaftafell. The visitor centre is 2 km down the road and has ample parking, as well as a very large campsite and extensive tourist facilities.

Hundafoss

River:	Skaðá in Bærjargil	Tiers:	1	
Facing:	SW	Height:	★★★	24 m
GPS:	64°01'11.9" N 16°58'49.6" W	Width:	★★	
(deg dec)	64.019978, -16.980443	Scenery:	★★★	

Description

Taking the Svartifoss trail in an anticlockwise direction, the first and highest of the falls is Hundafoss ('Dog falls'). This interesting waterfall gushes out of a tight undercut in the cliff walls and drops about 24 m in an expanding, continuously varying and almost pulsating plume of scintillating wavelets.

Despite its height and its location right on the trail, many hikers don't bother stopping to see Hundafoss. This is partly because it is half-hidden by abundant foliage — you need to squeeze through a few bushes to get a good vantage point. You can also get a clearer, if less interesting, view from the other side of the stream once you have been to Svartifoss, on the loop back to Skaftafell.

Directions

Starting from the visitor centre, follow the signposted Svartifoss trail past part of the camping area, then go sharply right and up a long series of steps. Hundafoss is about 850 m along the trail.

Hundafoss, viewed from the east side of the gorge, seems to pulsate as it falls 24 m from the cliff edge. GPS: 64°1'10" N 16°58'48" W (64.01944, -16.98000)

Magnúsarfoss

River:	Skaðá in Bærjargil	Tiers:	1	
Facing:	SE	Height:	★★	9 m
GPS:	64°01'16.0" N 16°58'47.9" W	Width:	★	
(deg dec)	64.021119, -16.979984	Scenery:	★★	

Description

Magnúsarfoss ('Magnus's Falls') is the second of the four waterfalls on the Svartifoss trail, and of modest height. Very few hikers seem to bother to stop to see it. This is partly because, like Hundafoss, it is a few metres off the main path and you need to push past the obscuring foliage to get a good view. It is hardly a gem but if you are on the trail why not have a look.

Directions

Follow the directions for Hundafoss. Magnúsarfoss is about 200 m past Hundafoss and just a few metres off the main trail.

Hikers often pass right by Magnúsarfoss but it is just off the trail to Svartifoss. GPS: 64°1'17" N 16°58'46" W (64.02139, -16.97944)

Svartifoss

River:	Skaðá in Bærjargil	Tiers:	1	
Facing:	SE	Height:	★★★	20 m
GPS:	64°01'39.6" N 16°58'31.1" W	Width:	★	
(deg dec)	64.027666, -16.975312	Scenery:	★★★ ½	

Description

Svartifoss ('Black Falls') is the third of the four waterfalls on the Svartifoss trail, and the one that attracts hordes of visitors every year. It is one of the most famous and most photographed of all the waterfalls in Iceland, although neither its height nor the volume of water flowing over it is at all striking.

Its name comes from the amphitheatre of black basalt columns behind it. This formation, seen all around the falls is perhaps the best example of columnar jointing in all of Iceland (along with Aldeyjarfoss), and is one of the most famous examples of the phenomenon on Earth. Other equally well-known formations can be seen at the Devil's Tower in Wyoming and the Giant's Causeway in Ireland. This distinction has led Svartifoss to be a much sought-after location for landscape photographers. It frequently appears in calendars featuring waterfalls, and is one of the most recognizable waterfalls in the world. Despite this, in terms of sheer beauty, Svartifoss is also probably the most overrated waterfall in Iceland.

From Svartifoss, many hikers return the way thay came, but a good alternative is to complete the loop by crossing the footbridge and taking the trail back down to the campsite, following the west side of the stream and always keeping to the left at three different forks. Along the way, you will pass good views of Hundafoss and Þjófafoss.

Taking the first right fork after the footbridge over the stream at Svartifoss will take you towards another waterfall, Skaðafoss, about 1.7 km upstream, to the north. However, adverse geological conditions may cause the park authorities to block the access.

Þjófafoss ('Thieves Falls') can be seen on the return trip from Svartifoss. It is the last of the four waterfalls on the Svartifoss trail, and of little height, 5 m. It is the least interesting of the Svartifoss trail waterfalls, and very few hikers bother to stop to see it. This is partly because it is a few metres off the main path and you need to push past the bushes to get a good view. It is perhaps worth a quick stop.

Directions

Svartifoss is about 750 m after Magnúsarfoss, along the Svartifoss trail. Svartifoss is at the top of the trail and about 1.8 km and a leisurely hour's walk from the visitor centre. You can get good views from either side of the footbridge crossing the stream.

Svartifoss, viewed from the footbridge over the stream. GPS: 64°01'36.7" N 16°58'29.8" W (64.02686, -16.97494)

A close view of the columnar basalt formations surrounding the waterfall. GPS: 64°1'38" N 16°58'31" W (64.02722, -16.97528)

Heygötufoss

River:	Eystrá	Tiers:	1
Facing:	W	Height:	★★
GPS:	64°01'16.3" N 16°58'22.2" W	Width:	★
(deg dec)	64.021204, -16.972832	Scenery:	★★★

Description

Most visitors to Skaftafell either ignore or do not even know of the existence of the delightful little gorge, Eystragil, that runs into the gorge of Bærjargil. The river within, which is possibly the Eystrá (but this is not certain), has several small but interesting waterfalls. Moreover, taking a quiet stroll along the gorge is a welcome change from tagging along with the majority on the often-crowded Svartifoss trail.

Heygötufoss is a lovely little waterfall, about 12 m high, nestled amongst the trees and rocks. Of particular interest is the contrast between the jet-black lava and basalt columns above the much clearer rock face and the lush greenery on the river banks.

If you venture further you will come across Austurheiðarfoss, really two waterfalls — Neðri-Austurheiðarfoss and Efri-Austurheiðarfoss — and two further pretty but unnamed falls.

Directions

Take the trail to Svartifoss. About 85 m before the first wooden bridge, take a small path to the right. It is about 700 m from the visitor centre. It may not be signposted and is not obvious. Heygötufoss is about 400 m from the junction with the Svartifoss trail.

Heygötufoss is nestled between rocks and lush vegetation. GPS: 64°1'16" N 16°58'25" W (64.02111, -16.97361)

Foss á Síðu (Síðufoss)

Region:	Suðurland (coastal)	Facing:	S		
Town:	Kirkjubæjarklaustur	Tiers:	2		
Area:	Kirkjubæjarklaustur	Height:	★ ★ ★ ★ ★	73+9 m
River:	Fossá	Width:	★ ★	3-7 m
GPS:	63°51'20.5" N 17°52'10.0" W	Scenery:	★ ★ ★	
(deg dec)	63.855702, -17.869445	Access:	2WD	Drive-up

Description

Foss á Síðu, literally 'The waterfall at Síðu', owes its claim to fame to its proximity to Route 1, and its great height, but certainly not to its river. The latter is little more than a stream, apparently not considered worthy of a name other than the near-universal 'Fossá'. The unusual form of the name seems to have stuck — you will rarely see the falls referred to as 'Síðufoss'.

You cannot fail to see the waterfall as you travel along Route 1 in either direction. The falls make a pretty picture, dropping off the top of a high cliff in a thin, straight plunge before glancing off bedrock, then broadening out for a second short step. Enormous boulders either side of the stream, and a third drop a little further down, complete the scenic setting. You cannot get very close to the waterfall, as it is on private land, but you do not need to, since the best view is from a distance.

Directions

Foss á Síðu is located off Route 1, about 11.3 km east of the roundabout at Kirkjubæjarklaustur. Signposts confirm the name of the very visible waterfall and you can park down a short gravel road, east of the bridge over the stream.

Foss á Síðu, viewed from Route 1 across the farm. GPS: 63°51'11" N 17°52'43" W (63.85306, -17.87861)

Stjórnarfoss

Region:	Suðurland (coastal)	Facing:	E		
Town:	Kirkjubæjarklaustur	Tiers:	2		
Area:	Kirkjubæjarklaustur	Height:	★★★	12+12 m	
River:	Stjórn	Width:	★★★	18 m	
GPS:	63°47'58.7" N 18°03'42.9" W	Scenery:	★★★★		
(deg dec)	63.855702, -17.869445	Access:	2WD	Drive-up	

Description

Stjórnarfoss ('Government Falls') is quite unique and difficult to classify. While moderate in size and height, it is a very scenic waterfall, in a charming setting of huge moss-covered protuberances of volcanic rock. The river is the Stjórn (surprisingly without the usual 'á' suffix).

Stjórnarfoss falls in two steps. The first tier is more of a sloping chute, while the second tier, some 50 m further down, cascades evenly over a dome-like tongue of basalt, creating an effect similar to a very large artificial water sculpture. At the base of the dome, the river broadens out and spreads itself over flat, beach-like banks of pebble and sand.

Directions

From the large roundabout that interrupts Route 1 at Kirkjubæjarklauster, turn north onto Route 203 (Geirlandsvegur) toward Geirland. It is about 1 km to the bridge over the Stjórn, with Stjórnarfoss plainly visible to the left. Park in the large open area on the other side of the bridge.

Cross the road and stay on the north side of the bridge. There is a path next to the Kleifer camping site, and you need to cross a stile and walk about 250 m in total to get close to the falls. You can only get a good view of both tiers by crossing the bridge over the river and hiking a little along the south bank.

The two tiers of Stjórnarfoss, viewed from the south side of the bridge. You can see a bench on the right. GPS: 63°48'3" N 18°3'21" W (63.80083, -18.05583)

Systrafoss

Region:	Suðurland (coastal)	Facing:	SE	
Town:	Kirkjubæjarklaustur	Tiers:	2	
Area:	Kirkjubæjarklaustur	Height:	★ ★ ★ ★	
River:	Fossá	Width:	★ ★	
GPS:	63°47'15.8" N 18°03'36.8" W	Scenery:	★ ★ ½	
(deg dec)	63.787713, -18.060231	Access:	2WD	Drive-up

Description

The proximity to Route 1, the pleasant village of Kirkjubæjarklaustur with its hotels and restaurants, the ease of access, and the waterfall's peculiar appearance are all good reasons why busloads of tourists often unload at the base of Systrafoss ('Sister's Falls').

The waterfall emanates from Lake Systravatn, which sits on a grassy plateau 100 m above the village. The name of the lake, 'Sister's Lake', derives from a story about two sisters of religion, or nuns. The two sisters from a nearby convent often went up to the lake to bathe. One day, two of them saw a hand wearing a fine golden ring emerge from the lake. They seized hold of the hand, and were dragged down into the depths.

Systrafoss slides in two parallel stripes some 70 m down a long bare incline of volcanic bedrock. About two thirds of the way down, an enormous outcrop further separates the two streams before they recombine amongst a jumble of boulders in the valley.

Directions

From the large roundabout that interrupts Route 1 at Kirkjubæjarklauster, turn west onto Route 205 (Klausturvegur) to the centre of the village. Continue west for 1.3 km to the Klaustur-Hof Guesthouse and Kaffi Munkar, where there is ample parking.

Systrafoss, seen from Route 1. GPS: 63°46'57" N 18°3'11" W (63.78250, -18.05306)

Mögáfoss

Region:	Suðurland (coastal)	Facing:	SE
Town:	Kirkjubæjarklaustur	Tiers:	1
Area:	Fjaðrárgljúfur	Height:	★★★★
River:	Mögá	Width:	★
GPS:	63°46' 45.7" N 18°10'43.4" W	Scenery:	★★★★ ½
(deg dec)	63.779357, -18.178725	Access:	2WD Easy

Description

Simply seen as a waterfall, Mögáfoss is not that amazing, but in the context of the spectacular canyon that surrounds it, it is spellbinding. (The waterfall has no definite name, but following Icelandic convention, its commonly-used name is derived from that of its river, the Mögá.) The falls descend about 35 m down a long incline of twisted, coloured rock and crash into the river Fjaðrá, deep within the canyon of Fjaðrárgljúfur.

To see the entire waterfall, you need to stand on a tiny promontory of rock some 100 m above the confluence of the two rivers, and look straight down. It is a spectacular view. Perhaps even more awe-inspiring is the view of the canyon looking south with the vista of deeply sculptured rocks, grassy slopes, sandy riverbed and flat, blue-tinged horizon.

Directions

From the large roundabout that interrupts Route 1 at Kirkjubæjarklauster, drive 6 km south-west on Route 1 to the signposted turnoff to Fjaðrárgljúfur canyon, on Route 206 (Holtsvegur). Continue for 2.3 km past the fork for Route F206 and after another 1 km you will reach a small car park with an information panel for Fjaðrárgljúfur canyon. You should follow the canyon rim to get to to the waterfall, a distance of about 1 km, and fully appreciate the many wonderful views along the way.

Looking almost straight down at Mögáfoss. GPS: 63°46'44" N 18°10'35" W (63.77889, -18.17639)

Fagrifoss

Region:	Suðurland (coastal)	Facing:	S	
Town:	Kirkjubæjarklaustur	Tiers:	1	
Area:	Lakagígar	Height:	★ ★ ★ ★ ★	
River:	Geirlandsá	Width:	★ ★ ★ ★	
GPS:	63°52'06.0" N 18°14'46.4" W	Scenery:	★ ★ ★ ★ ★	
(deg dec)	63.868342, -18.246214	Access:	4WD	Easy

Description

Fagrifoss ('Beautiful Falls') is one of the most stunning waterfalls in Iceland, although not everyone can easily see it because of its remoteness. You need a high, heavy 4WD vehicle to get there since you have to cross a couple of fords, one of which is the very river that feeds the waterfall. Fagrifoss is located off F206, on the road to the Laki craters, and is an obligatory stop for guided tours from Kirkjubæjarklaustur to Lakagígar. It falls some 70 m in two main chutes separated by an enormous tongue of rock. Each channel crashes into equally large outcrops on the way down, resulting in a magnificent spectacle of spidery streamers fanning out in all directions.

Directions

From the large roundabout that interrupts Route 1 at Kirkjubæjarklauster, drive 6 km south-west on Route 1 to the signposted turnoff to Fjaðrárgljúfur canyon on Route 206 (Holtsvegur). Continue for 2.3 km and take the fork for Route F206. Although the first part of the road is desceptively easy, it soon becomes quite rough and is only suitable for 4WD vehicles. F206 is closed for most of the year, and may only be opened for a few short summer months. You will need to drive about 24 km, crossing a stream and a small river in the process, before you come to a major ford over the Geirlandsá. Beware, light 4WD vehicles may not be able to cross. It is about 500 m further to a parking area.

It is only a short walk to the rim of the canyon above Fagrifoss. There is also a specially constructed belvedere a few metres higher up the mountain where you can take in the full view of Fagrifoss and the river Geirlandsá, above and below the falls.

Fagrifoss. A magnificent spectacle of spidery streamers fanning out in all directions. GPS: 63°52'7" N 18°14'41" W (63.86861, -18.24472)

Skógafoss

Region:	Suðurland (coastal)	Facing:	SW	
Town:	Hvolsvöllur	Tiers:	1	
Area:	Skógaheiði	Height:	★ ★ ★ ★ ★	60-70 m
River:	Skógá	Width:	★ ★ ★ ½	25-30 m
GPS:	63°31'55.7" N 19°30'40.5" W	Scenery:	★ ★ ★ ★ ★	
(deg dec)	63.532131, -19.511253	Access:	2WD	Drive-up

Description

Skógafoss is a must-see for any visitor to Iceland. It is one of the best waterfalls in the country and probably the most visited since it is also so easily accessible.

According to legend, the first Viking settler in the area, Þrasi Þórólfsson, buried a treasure in a cave behind the waterfall. Locals found the chest years later, but were only able to grasp the ring on the side before the chest disappeared again. The ring was allegedly given to the local church. The old church door ring is now in a museum, although whether this adds veracity to the folklore is debatable. 'Skógafoss' means 'Forest Falls' or 'Forest River Falls' after its river, Skógá.

The Skógá stems from the runoff between the Eyjafjallajökull and Mýrdalsjökull glaciers. Its final plunge off the broad plateau is a spectactular vertical drop of between 60 and 70 m, across a straight edge of between 25 and 30 m, shouldered by rounded cliffs on either side. (Surprisingly, despite its fame, there are no definite dimensions for Skógafoss. Even the sign at the base of the falls somehow claims the width is 15 m, which it most certainly is not.) As the water hits the bedrock below, it sends huge clouds of spray and mist into the air. This makes it difficult to get very close to the waterfall but the best views are from a distance anyway, especially when there are a few people near the base to show off the scale and immense size of the falls.

A quite different view involves considerable exertion to climb the hundreds of steps up a specially constructed staircase all the way to the top, where there is a good viewing platform. From there you can look over the town of Skogar and trace the river to where it joins the sea, 5 km to the south. Allow an hour to walk the 600 m from the car park to the top and back, with stops for taking in the views.

See the following section on Skógá waterfalls for information on a popular hike that starts at Skógafoss and takes in over 20 beautiful waterfalls along the river Skógá.

Directions

From the town of Hvolsvöllur, drive east on Route 1 for 47 km, and turn where signs indicate Skógafoss. You can hardly miss seeing the waterfall from the road. (If you are coming from Selfoss, it is about 98 km going west on Route 1.) Take the first left and follow the road to the car park near the vast camping area. There are toilet and washing facilities within the camp site.

Skógafoss dwarfs the surrounding landscape. The staircase to the right leads you up hundreds of steps to a view above the falls. GPS: 63°31'34" N 19°31'15" W (63.52611, -19.52083)

Skógafoss drops over 60 m and sends clouds of spray into the air. GPS: 63°31'49" N 19°30'47" W (63.53028, -19.51306)

Skógá Waterfalls

Region:	Suðurland (coastal)
Town:	Hvolsvöllur
Area:	Skógaheiði

Access: 2WD Easy to Vigorous

Description

The so-called Fimmvörðuháls ('Five-Cairn') trail is one of the most popular long hikes in Iceland. It is a one- or two-day hike of over 25 km from Skogar to Þórsmörk over the pass between the Eyjafjallajökull and Myrdalsjökull glaciers. The first part of the hike starts at Skógafoss and follows the Skógá upriver, passing many wonderful waterfalls in about 8 km with a change in elevation of nearly 600 m. This section ends at a footbridge over the Skógá, and is often completed as a shorter Skógá Waterfalls hike taking four to six hours for the round trip. The number of waterfalls along the route depends on how you count them and different sources put it as between 22 and 28 falls, this guide assumes 25. However, not all are easily observable from the trail and many do not have names.

The table below and following sub-sections summarise those that are significant falls along the route, with most of these worthy of a stop and admiration:

No.	Name	Description	GPS Coordinates
1	Skógafoss	One of the most visited waterfalls in Iceland. Over 60 m high and 25 m wide.	63°31'55.7" N 19°30'40.5" W (63.532131, -19.511253)
2	Hestavaðsfoss	A lovely two-tiered very broad waterfall with a total height of about 9 m.	63°31'59.6" N 19°30'26.8" W (63.533215, -19.507442)
3	Fosstorfufoss	A distinctive waterfall, breaking into two parts at 90° to one another.	63°32'07.6" N 19°30'08.5" W (63.535444, -19.502352)
4	Steinbogafoss	A simple block waterfall of about 8 m height in a picturesque setting.	63°32'16.4" N 19°30'07.6" W (63.537900, -19.502113)
5	Unamed (Skógá No. 5)	Minor rapids, dropping about 6 m over a series of ledges, and a distance of about 30 m.	63°32'20.2" N 19°30'08.3" W (63.538944, -19.502319)
6	Fremri-Fellsfoss	A moderately sized square-shaped waterfall of about 15 m in height.	63°32'35.5" N 19°29'59.9" W (63.543187, -19.499983)
7	Innri-Fellsfoss	Similar to Fremri-Fellsfoss but twice as wide.	63°32'40.1" N 19°30'05.6" W (63.544482, -19.50154)
8	Rollutorfufoss	Resembling a natural weir, diagonally across the river. About 37 m wide.	63°32'43.9" N 19°30'02.7" W (63.545536, -19.500750)
9	Skálabrekkufoss	The second or third highest waterfall on the river. It falls	63°32'55.5" N 19°29'44.8" W (63.548760, -19.495772)

		over 40 m into a narrow chasm.	
10	Kæfufoss	A magnificent waterfall in a broad T shape, spanning the river in two sections. About 14 m high and 25 to 35 m across.	63°32'57.6" N 19°29'41.2" W (63.549333, -19.494785)
11	Unamed (Skógá No. 11)	A small waterfall 100 m upriver from Kæfufoss and half-hidden round a bend with difficult access. Visible from above Kæfufoss.	63°33'01.4" N 19°29'42.5" W (63.550375, -19.495142)
12	Unamed Tributary (Skógá No. 12)	A delightful little waterfall that pours into the Skógá from a small stream on the east bank of the river.	63°33'12.9" N 19°29'29.9" W (63.553572, -19.491644)
13	Unamed (Skógá No. 13)	A small waterfall very deep down in a narrow chasm. There is no access and it is difficult to obtain a good view from the cliff top.	63°33'28.0" N 19°29'32.4" W (63.557767, -19.492342)
14	Unamed (Skógá No. 14)	Very similar to the above. A small waterfall very deep down in a narrow chasm. There is no access and it is difficult to obtain a good view from the cliff top.	63°33'36.1" N 19°29'28.0" W (63.560018, -19.491103)
15	Gluggafoss	An interesting waterfall deep within the gorge that is split into three streams by a huge rock. About 12 m high by 15 m wide.	63°33'39.7" N 19°29'21.6" W (63.561024, -19.489338)
16	Unamed (Skógá No. 16)	A low, turbulent and elongated waterfall very deep down in a narrow chasm. There is no access and it is difficult to obtain a good view from the cliff top. The best views are from upriver looking back down the canyon.	63°33'46.3" N 19°29'19.9" W (63.562858, -19.488861)
17	Króksfoss	The second or third highest waterfall on the river. It falls over 40 m into a narrow chasm.	63°33'53.9" N 19°29'27.3" W (63.564962, -19.490926)
18	Hornfell Foss	A lovely little waterfall from a tributary to the Skógá river, coming down from Hornfell mountain.	63°33'58.5" N 19°29'26.1" W (63.566247, -19.490572)

19	Unamed (Skógá No. 19)	Similar in form to Króksfoss, but half as high. Situated in a picturesque gorge.	63°33'59.6" N 19°29'21.1" W (63.566550, -19.489183)
20	Unamed (Skógá No. 20)	A moderately-sized square-shaped waterfall. However, neither it nor the surrounding scenery is noteworthy.	63°34'01.2" N 19°29'17.5" W (63.566994, -19.488191)
21	Unamed (Skógá No. 21)	An interesting curtain waterfall, twice as high as it is wide. A tributary joins it at the top.	63°34'17.4" N 19°28'23.6" W (63.571489, -19.473230)
22	Unamed (Skógá No. 22)	Similar to Rollutorfufoss. Resembling a low natural weir placed diagonally across the river.	63°34'18.8" N 19°28'06.5" W (63.571885, -19.468466)
23	Neðstifoss	The lower half of a twin set of waterfalls. On its own it is not very impressive, but combined with Miðfoss it is fantastic.	63°34'31.2" N 19°27'12.4" W (63.575347, -19.453456)
24	Miðfoss	The upper half of a twin set of waterfalls. On its own it is majestic, and combined with Neðstifoss it is fantastic.	63°34'31.8" N 19°27'07.0" W (63.575485, -19.451933)
25	Efstifoss	A magnificent curtain waterfall that plunges over 30 m into a cavernous amphitheatre.	63°34'31.4" N 19°26'57.9" W (63.575380, -19.449412)

Directions

Follow the directions for Skógafoss. The trail starts at the top of the waterfall.

Hestavaðsfoss

River:	Skógá		Tiers:	2	
Facing:	SW		Height:	★★	3+6 m
GPS:	63°31'59.6" N 19°30'26.8" W		Width:	★★★★★	
(deg dec)	63.533215, -19.507442		Scenery:	★★★★	

Description

Hestavaðsfoss is a lovely two-tiered, very broad waterfall just above Skógafoss. It stretches over 50 m across the river at its widest point. Like most of the falls along the trail, it is easily seen from the hiking path.

Directions

From the top of Skógafoss, climb over the twisted stile and take the path following the river for about 250 m.

The view of broad Hestavaðsfoss provides a magnificent vista. GPS: 63°31'58" N 19°30'30" W (63.53278, -19.50833)

Fosstorfufoss

River:	Skógá		Tiers:	1	
Facing:	SW-NW		Height:	★ ★	10 m
GPS:	63°32'07.6" N 19°30'08.5" W		Width:	★ ★ ★ ★ ½	
(deg dec)	63.535444, -19.502352		Scenery:	★ ★ ★ ★	

Description

Fosstorfufoss is a picturesque and distinctive waterfall a little above Hestavaðsfoss. It falls about 10 m in two cascades at 90° to one another, forming a bend in the river in the process. Its overall width, summing each independent section, is around 50 m. The many large boulders above and below the falls complete a very scenic view.

Directions

Fosstorfufoss is about 400 m further along the path from Hestavaðsfoss.

Fosstorfufoss breaks into two cascades at 90° to each other. GPS: 63°32'7" N 19°30'13" W (63.53528, -19.50361)

Steinbogafoss

River:	Skógá		Tiers:	1	
Facing:	SE		Height:	★★	8 m
GPS:	63°32'16.4" N 19°30'07.6" W		Width:	★★★	20 m
(deg dec)	63.537900, -19.502113		Scenery:	★★★	

Description

Steinbogafoss is a simple, block-shaped waterfall a little above Fosstorfufoss. Although Steinbogafoss is not very amazing in its own right, the depth of the gorge at this point and the mountains in the distance make a nice picture. 'Steinbogafoss' means 'Stone Arch Falls' but there is no history or legend that explains the name.

Directions

Steinbogafoss is about 450 m from Fosstorfufoss.

Steinbogafoss, Skógá and mountains. GPS: 63°32'12" N 19°30'1" W (63.53667, -19.50028)

Fremri-Fellsfoss

River:	Skógá	Tiers:	1
Facing:	S	Height:	★★★ 15 m
GPS:	63°32'35.5" N 19°29'59.9" W	Width:	★★★ 17 m
(deg dec)	63.543187, -19.499983	Scenery:	★★★

Description

Fremri-Fellsfoss ('Outer Fell Falls') is a moderately-sized block waterfall about 1.75 km above Skógafoss. The river plunges into a hard rock basin, producing quite a lot of noise and spray that can climb high into the air. Fremri-Fellsfoss is followed by Innri-Fellsfoss ('Inner Fell Falls') 100 m further up. The latter is similar in height to its sister waterfall, although much broader. It is difficult to approach closely for a full view.

Directions

Fremri-Fellsfoss is about 650 m from Steinbogafoss.

Fremri-Fellsfoss, with Innri-Fellsfoss in the distance. GPS: 63°32'33" N 19°29'58" W (63.54250, -19.49944)

Rollutorfufoss

River:	Skógá		Tiers:	1	
Facing:	S		Height:	★	5 m
GPS:	63°32'43.9" N 19°30'02.7" W		Width:	★ ★ ★ ★	37 m
(deg dec)	63.545536, -19.500750		Scenery:	★ ★ ★	

Description

Rollutorfufoss is so unimpressive in height that it is hard to imagine that the same river becomes the magnificent Skógafoss. However, the lovely gorge, the falls' diagonal orientation and breadth across the river, and the rocks strewn all about, create a certain charm.

Directions

Rollutorfufoss is about 100 m from Innri-Fellsfoss and nearly 2 km from Skógafoss.

Rollutorfufoss resembles a natural weir placed diagonally across the river. GPS: 63°32'43" N 19°30'1" W (63.54528, -19.50028)

Skálabrekkufoss

River:	Skógá		Tiers:	1	
Facing:	SW		Height:	★★★★	43 m
GPS:	63°32'55.5" N 19°29'44.8" W		Width:	★★★	18 m
(deg dec)	63.548760, -19.495772		Scenery:	★★★	

Description

Skálabrekkufoss is a majestic waterfall. It is the second or third highest waterfall on the Skógá river, after Skógafoss, and similar in height to Króksfoss. Here the river launches off a high cliff and thunders over 40 m down into a deep, slot-like chasm. It is not easy to approach the waterfall or get a full view as the ravine is very deep, steep and tortuous. You need to leave the trail and venture sometimes precariously close to the rim's edge to get a good view. Incidentally, interesting rainbows are often created because of the large amounts of spray and angle of the falls relative to the sun.

Directions

Skálabrekkufoss is about 550 m from Rollutorfufoss and about 2.5 km from Skógafoss.

Thunder and spray from Skálabrekkufoss as it drops over 40 m into the chasm. GPS: 63°32'53" N 19°29'49" W (63.54806, -19.49694)

Kæfufoss

River:	Skógá		Tiers:	1	
Facing:	SW		Height:	★ ★ ★	14 m
GPS:	63°32'57.6" N 19°29'41.2" W		Width:	★ ★ ★ ★	25-35 m
(deg dec)	63.549333, -19.494785		Scenery:	★ ★ ★ ★	

Description

Kæfufoss is a magnificent waterfall in a highly picturesque setting. It has a unique T form, with half the falls perpendicular to the other half that lies diagonally across the river. Kæfufoss uniquely has one tier on one side and two or three tiers on the other. Its width depends on how it is measured. No matter, it is a fantastic sight that is enhanced by the way the river bends around and between massive boulders fallen from the canyon walls on each side.

From your vantage point overlooking Kæfufoss you can also look back from what is the top of Skálabrekkufoss down the canyon towards the south. It is a lovely view.

Directions

Kæfufoss is only about 250 m from Skálabrekkufoss and about 2.75 km from Skógafoss.

Kæfufoss is a magnificent sight. GPS: 63°32'55" N 19°29'42" W (63.54861, -19.49500)

Gluggafoss

River:	Skógá		Tiers:	1	
Facing:	W		Height:	★★	12 m
GPS:	63°33'39.7" N 19°29'21.6" W		Width:	★★★	15 m
(deg dec)	63.561024, -19.489338		Scenery:	★★★ ½	

Description

Gluggafoss is an interesting waterfall, split into three streams by a huge rock that very nearly dams the river at this point. The rock has a hole in it through which the middle stream gushes, hence the name meaning 'Window Falls'.

The gorge is interesting here, too. The vantage point is high above the Skógá, and the view now opens out again after passing a section of the trail where the river virtually disappeared into the depths of the narrow canyon far below.

Directions

Gluggafoss is about 1.45 km from Kæfufoss, and about 4.2 km from Skógafoss. Unlike most of the preceding waterfalls, which are closely packed and easily seen, it takes a little more effort and a good climb to reach Gluggafoss.

Gluggafoss is split into three streams by two huge rocks. GPS: 63°33'38" N 19°29'22" W (63.56056, -19.48944)

Króksfoss

River:	Skóga	Tiers:	3		
Facing:	SE	Height:	★★★★	44 m	
GPS:	63°33'53.9" N 19°29'27.3" W	Width:	★★★	20 m	
(deg dec)	63.564962, -19.490926	Scenery:	★★★★		

Description

Króksfoss is an imposing three-tiered waterfall. Similar in height to Skálabrekkufoss, it is the second or third highest waterfall on the Skógá river, after Skógafoss. Unlike the former, you can get right up to it, that is to say above and in front of it. From the cliff top opposite, you can watch the river reach the edge of the first tier, then drop slightly before plummeting off into space in a broad fan of wavelets. It is a fascinating spectacle. You also get a wonderful view down the canyon from this point, and, since you can walk to the top of the waterfall, you can get a great view from there as well.

Directions

Króksfoss is about 600 m from Gluggafoss and about 4.8 km from Skógafoss.

Króksfoss breaks into wavelets as it plummets 44 m down into the canyon. GPS: 63°33'54" N 19°29'26" W (63.56500, -19.49056)

Hornfell Foss

River:	Unknown		Tiers:	1
Facing:	S		Height:	★ ★ ★
GPS:	63°33'58.5" N 19°29'26.1" W		Width:	★
(deg dec)	63.566247, -19.490572		Scenery:	★ ★ ½

Description

Hornfell Foss is on an unnamed tributary to the Skógá coming down from Hornfell Mountain on the west side of the river. It is a lovely, little waterfall. If you scramble down the slope to the water below, you will find a great sheltered spot for a rest or picnic.

Directions

Hornfell Foss is about 100 m from Króksfoss and about 4.9 km from Skógafoss.

Hornfell Foss is a lovely little waterfall from a tributary to the Skógá. GPS: 63°33'56" N 19°29'26" W (63.56556, -19.49056)

Unnamed waterfall (Skógá No. 19)

River:	Skógá		Tiers:	2
Facing:	SW		Height:	★ ★ ★
GPS:	63°33'59.6" N 19°29'21.1" W		Width:	★ ★
(deg dec)	63.566550, -19.489183		Scenery:	★ ★ ★

Description

This unnamed two-tiered waterfall is worthy of a stop – and a name. The Skógá winds its way down the picturesque gorge before pouring down some 20 to 25 m into a frothing circular basin. The waterfall itself is similar to Króksfoss in form, although nowhere near as high.

Directions

The waterfall is about 100 m from Hornfell Foss, 200 m from Króksfoss, and about 5 km from Skógafoss.

This unnamed waterfall is number 19 along the waterfall trail and worthy of a stop and a name. GPS: 63°33'59" N 19°29'23" W (63.56639, -19.48972)

Unnamed waterfall (Skógá No. 20)

River:	Skógá	Tiers:	1
Facing:	W	Height:	★ ★ ★
GPS:	63°34'01.2" N 19°29'17.5" W	Width:	★ ★ ★
(deg dec)	63.566994, -19.488191	Scenery:	★ ★ ½

Description

This unnamed, very square-shaped block waterfall is easily seen from the trail. While of a respectable size, neither it nor the surrounding scenery is particularly noteworthy. When compared to the many beautiful waterfalls along the river it is relatively unimpressive.

Directions

The waterfall is about 200 m from Skógá No. 19 and about 5.2 km from Skógafoss.

Unnamed waterfall number 20 along the Skógá river. GPS: 63°34'1" N 19°29'18" W (63.56694, -19.48833)

Unnamed waterfall (Skógá No. 21)

River:	Skógá	Tiers:	1
Facing:	W	Height:	★ ★ ★
GPS:	63°34'17.4" N 19°28'23.6" W	Width:	★ ★
(deg dec)	63.571489, -19.473230	Scenery:	★ ★ ★

Description

This unnamed curtain waterfall is easily seen from the trail. About twice as tall as it is wide, it falls into a steeply-sided amphitheatre, hitting some large boulders at its base. The surrounding scenery is pleasant and there is an additional touch in the form of a small tributary that joins the Skógá just before the falls.

Directions

The waterfall is about 800 m from Skógá No. 20 and about 6 km from Skógafoss.

Unnamed waterfall number 21 along the Skógá river. GPS: 63°34'17" N 19°28'29" W (63.57139, -19.47472)

Unnamed waterfall (Skógá No. 22)

River:	Skógá	Tiers:	1
Facing:	S	Height:	★★
GPS:	63°34'18.8" N 19°28'06.5" W	Width:	★★★★
(deg dec)	63.571885, -19.468466	Scenery:	★★★

Description

This unnamed waterfall is similar to Rollutorfufoss. It resembles a low, natural weir placed diagonally across the river.

Directions

The waterfall is about 400 m from Skógá No. 21 and about 6.4 km from Skógafoss.

Unnamed waterfall number 22 along the Skógá river. GPS: 63°34'17" N 19°28'10" W (63.57139, -19.46944)

Neðstifoss

River:	Skóga	Tiers:	1	
Facing:	W	Height:	★★	
GPS:	63°34'31.2" N 19°27'12.4" W	Width:	★★	
(deg dec)	63.575347, -19.453456	Scenery:	★★★	

Description

Neðstifoss ('Bottom Falls') is a modestly sized, block waterfall, invariably associated with its much more imposing sister, Miðfoss, that looms just behind it. Were it not for the overall perspective of both waterfalls in their spectacular, fantasy-like canyon, this waterfall would hardly be worth a mention.

Directions

The waterfall is about 1 km from Skóga No. 22 and about 7.4 km from Skógafoss.

Neðstifoss in front with Miðfoss behind. The canyon is spectacular. GPS: 63°34'31" N 19°27'19" W (63.57528, -19.45528)

Miðfoss

River:	Skógá		Tiers:	1
Facing:	W		Height:	★ ★ ★
GPS:	63°34'31.8" N 19°27'07.0" W		Width:	★ ★
(deg dec)	63.575485, -19.451933		Scenery:	★ ★ ★ ★

Description

Miðfoss ('Middle Falls') is the one of the highest waterfalls on the Skógá river. Although good estimates of its height are lacking, the combined height of Miðfoss and Neðstifoss is thought to be about 25 m. The waterfall plunges off an overhang and splashes into a small pool at its base. The veil-like form and skinny aspect ratio of Miðfoss, along with the stunning contours of the canyon surrounding it, give it a mysterious almost magical aura.

Directions

Miðfoss is about 200 m from Neðstifoss, and about 7.6 km from Skógafoss.

Miðfoss has a mysterious, almost magical aura about it. GPS: 63°34'31" N 19°27'19" W (63.57528, -19.45528)

Efstifoss

River:	Skógá	Tiers:	1	
Facing:	NW	Height:	★ ★ ★ ★	
GPS:	63°34'31.4" N 19°26'57.9" W	Width:	★ ★ ★	
(deg dec)	63.575380, -19.449412	Scenery:	★ ★ ★ ★ ½	

Description

At nearly 600 m in elevation, Efstifoss ('Top Falls') is the anchor at the end of the chain of waterfalls along the Skógá trail that begins with Skógafoss. It is almost as imposing as Skógafoss, although in a very different way. It is truly magnificent. The river pours over a ledge of deeply tortured lava to plunge more than 30 m into a large amphitheatre with turquoise water at the bottom, and very often snow around the sides. Unfortunately, without a person in the picture, it is very difficult to appreciate the scale and size of Efstifoss.

For those who want to see even more waterfalls, or just want to hike further into the highlands, you can continue on the Fimmvörðuháls trail to Þórsmörk. The path passes over a wooden footbridge that marks the end of the Skógá Waterfalls trail, but there are at least a further ten waterfalls along the way, including Slæðufoss, a lovely, low-lying, fan-shaped waterfall, about 1.5 km from the bridge.

Directions

Efstifoss is about 200 m from Miðfoss and about 7.8 km from Skógafoss.

Magnificent Efstifoss falls over 30 m down into a vast amphitheatre. GPS: 63°34'31" N 19°27'3" W (63.57528, -19.45083)

Kvernufoss

Region:	Suðurland (coastal)	Facing:	SW	
Town:	Hvolsvöllur	Tiers:	1	
Area:	Skógaheiði	Height:	★★★	
River:	Kverná	Width:	★	
GPS:	63°31'42.9" N 19°28'50.1" W	Scenery:	★★★	
(deg dec)	63.528581, -19.480575	Access:	2WD	Easy

Description

Kvernufoss sits half-hidden in a charming glen, not far from the Skógar museum. Although thousands of sightseers flock to Skógafoss, it is surprising that almost no one bothers to see Kvernufoss. It is a wonderful reward for those who make the short walk.

The Kverná pours off a ledge overhanging a cavernous hollow in the cliff, drops straight down nearly 20 m, and splashes into a shallow, stony pool. You can easily walk round the waterfall for an interesting view from behind.

Directions

Follow the directions for Skógafoss. When on the access road do not turn left towards the waterfall but head straight on. Turn right towards the excellent Skógar Museum, pass it and go as far as you can, then park behind a farm building close by some rusting antique farm equipment.

Go over the stile and head towards the river, where you will pick up a trail. Follow the path to the base of the waterfall. It is about 600 m in all.

Kvernufoss splashes down into a cavernous hollow in a charming glen, forming a column of light in the darkness. GPS: 63°31'39" N 19°28'54" W (63.52750, -19.48167)

Seljalandsfoss

Region:	Suðurland (coastal)	Facing:	NW		
Town:	Hvolsvöllur	Tiers:	1		
Area:	Seljelandsheiði	Height:	★ ★ ★ ★ ★	60-65 m	
River:	Seljalandsá	Width:	★ ★ ½	10-15 m	
GPS:	63°36'56.3" N 19°59'16.6" W	Scenery:	★ ★ ★ ★		
(deg dec)	63.615639, -19.987945	Access:	2WD	Drive-up	

Description

Seljalandsfoss ('Angel Falls') ranks as one of the most famous, accessible, and most visited of Iceland's waterfalls. Not only is it about the same height as Skógafoss, but it is also fairly close to it, making it a must stop on the tourist circuit. In fairness, Seljalandsfoss is a beautiful and exceptional waterfall, and well worth the accolades given to it. Its uniqueness comes from the extensive overhang formed by the cliff top and the large hollowed-out undercut near its base. The broad cascade forms a curtain behind which a wide path allows sightseers to traverse the entire width of the waterfall while remaining several metres away from it. The views from in front, the sides and behind the falls are equally varied and fascinating.

The only drawbacks to Seljalandsfoss — and they are considerable — are the spray, the wind, and the vast hordes of visitors. Like Skógafoss, when water falls 60 m over a wide breadth into a large pool, there is going to be a lot of spray. Add the usual amount of fluctuating wind, and if you are standing to the side or just behind the waterfall, you are likely to get drenched. It also makes it very difficult to take pictures. As for the third inconvenience — the thousands of tourists, along with many, many cars and buses overflowing the small car park and lining the road for hundreds of metres - you will have to live with that as a necessary price of admission. If you can, try to go late in the afternoon when there are relatively fewer people and there is still good sunlight from the north-westerly exposure.

There are two minor falls to the north. A pleasant walk over the wooden footbridge takes you on a trail that leads you past them and on to the wonderful Gljúfrafoss 600 m further on (see the next entry).

Directions

From the town of Hvolsvöllur, drive east on Route 1 for a little over 20 km to Route 249 (Þórsmerkurvegur). The road is signposted for Seljalandsfoss and Þórsmörk. At this point it is difficult to miss Seljalandsfoss as it is so large and so close. It is 730 m to the entrance of the car park.

You can get a good view from near the car park, but a short walk rewards you with many different views. If you are adequately waterproofed, head to the right and then all the way behind and round the waterfall coming out on the left.

Seljalandsfoss in all its magnificence. Note the people standing in the undercut behind the waterfall. GPS: 63°36'57" N 19°59'24" W (63.61583, -19.99000)

A view from behind and to the right of the falls, and only slightly beyond the reach of the spray. GPS: 63°36'54" N 19°59'18" W (63.61500, -19.98833)

Gljúfrafoss
(Gljúfurárfoss, Gljúfrabúi, Hamragarðafoss)

Region:	Suðurland (coastal)	Facing:	NW	
Town:	Hvolsvöllur	Tiers:	1	
Area:	Hamragarðaheiði	Height:	★ ★ ★ ★	40 m
River:	Gljúfurá	Width:	★	5 m
GPS:	63°37'15.3" N 19°59'08.3" W	Scenery:	★ ★ ★ ★	
(deg dec)	63.620926, -19.985638	Access:	2WD	Easy

Description

It is only a short walk from Seljalandsfoss to Gljúfrafoss, but the latter is far less well-known. The main reason is that it is very difficult to see. The Gljúfurá is a small spring-fed stream, which falls into a deep chasm whose exit is blocked by a huge palagonite boulder that forms part of the Franskanef cliff. This gives the impression that Gljúfrafoss comes out of a cave. Only the very top is visible from outside.

Gljúfrafoss can be translated as 'Canyon Falls' but a more meaningful interpretation would be 'Chasm River Falls'. Gljúfurárfoss or Gljúfrabúi are commonly used alternative names for the waterfall, but the locals often call it Hamragarðafoss after the ancient farmstead Hamragarðar on which land it is situated.

Directions

From the town of Hvolsvöllur, drive east on Route 1 for a little over 20 km to Route 249 (Þórsmerkurvegur). The road is signposted for Seljalandsfoss and Þórsmörk. Drive past Seljalandsfoss for 1.4 km to the entrance of the Hamragarðar Camping Ground. Preferably park just outside the campsite entrance. Only park inside, to the left by the stream if there is ample room in the field, so as not to disturb the occupants.

From inside the campsite, it is only a few metres to where the stream flows out from between the rock walls. There are two ways to see the waterfall, both a little hazardous. The 'interior' method requires wading into the stream, or carefully stepping from rock to rock, and then getting drenched by the spray as Gljúfrafoss channels down the cliff faces and splashes over the rocks below. In the centre of the surprisingly spacious area there is a round boulder that makes a great viewing and photo spot for the well-protected or impervious adventurer. The 'exterior' method involves a steep climb that can be very slippery, using an anchored chain for support, then climbing a wooden ladder to get halfway up the waterfall for a fabulous view.

Gljúfrafoss pours and splatters down from on high. GPS: 63°37'15" N 19°59'10" W (63.62083, -19.98611)

Gluggafoss
(Gluggárfoss, Merkjárfoss, Merkifoss)

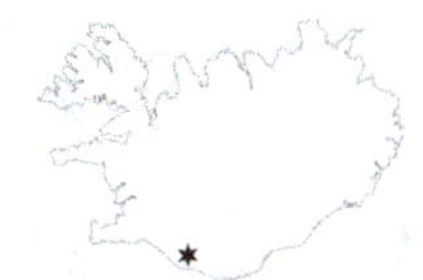

Region:	Suðurland (coastal)	Facing:	S	
Town:	Hvolsvöllur	Tiers:	2	
Area:	Fljótshlíð	Height:	★ ★ ★ ★ ★	45+8m
River:	Merkjá	Width:	★ ★ ★	5-18 m
GPS:	63°43'15.8" N 19°53'33.1" W	Scenery:	★ ★ ★ ½	
(deg dec)	63.721056, -19.892531	Access:	2WD	Drive-up

Description

Gluggafoss is composed of two very different tiers separated by a large pool. The upper tier drains off soft palagonite rock while the lower tier is on basalt. Over time, the river has carved a series of tunnels and grooves in the palagonite that opened out into several windows, hence the name 'Gluggafoss' meaning 'Windows Falls'. Before 1947, you could barely see the upper half of the waterfall as the water disappeared into a vertical tunnel within the cliff. It was only visible through three openings, one above the other. The water emerged through the bottom window, which then formed an arch. At times of flooding, water gushed out of all three windows.

In 1947, the volcano Hekla erupted, carrying a thick layer of ash into the tunnels, nearly blocking them completely and forcing the water to flow over the top. Gradually over the years, erosion has started to remove the sediment and unblock the tunnels. There is now a stone arch at the very top of the waterfall.

Gluggafoss is also called Merkjárfoss, or the slightly shortened Merkifoss, after the river Merkjá. The lower tier is sometimes called Hverfifoss.

The waterfall faces south, but due to its deep recess into the cliff it is likely to be in partial shadow most of the day. The best time to see the falls is around mid-day.

Very nearby, there are two other interesting waterfalls, Þórðarfoss and Drífandi (see the next entry). From Gluggafoss you can take a path heading west. There is also a farm track from the parking area. These lead you to Þórðarfoss, just 230 m away, and Drífandi, 600 m further on.

Directions

From the town of Hvolsvöllur, drive east on Route 261 (Fljótshlíðarvegur) for 17.3 km to where the road crosses the Merkjá below the waterfall. A sign indicates the parking area for Gluggafoss. Alternatively, coming from Seljelandsfoss and the junction 1/249, continue on Route 1 for 4.5 km to the junction with Route 250 (Hólmabæjavegur). Take this road for 12 km to the junction with Route 261, which almost faces the waterfall.

Although you have a good view of Gluggafoss from the parking area, a short easy walk takes you right to the lower tier, where there are steps leading to the pool above it and closer to the upper tier.

Gluggafoss emerges from a stone arch at the top and is half-hidden by the cliff. GPS: 63°43'11" N 19°53'34" W (63.71972, -19.89278)

The lower tier of Gluggafoss, sometimes called Hverfifoss. It is not as small as appears from a distance. It is 8 m high. GPS: 63°43'14.7"N 19°53'35.1"W (63.72075, -19.89308)

Drífandi (Drífandifoss)

Region:	Suðurland (coastal)	Facing:	S
Town:	Hvolsvöllur	Tiers:	1
Area:	Þorsteinslundur, Fljótshlíð	Height:	★ ★ ★ ★
River:	Unknown	Width:	★
GPS:	63°43'17.8" N 19°54'31.3" W	Scenery:	★ ★ ★ ½
(deg dec)	63.721612, -19.908691	Access:	2WD Drive-up

Description

Drífandi drops into the idyllic, sheltered wood and park of Þorsteinslundur. The park is dedicated to Þorsteinn Erlingsson, a popular nineteenth century Icelandic poet. It is a wonderful, almost magical glade, and the tall, skinny Drífandi adds to the fairy-tale feel of the place as the breeze tugs and twists it, sending wisps dancing away and back again. Needless to say, it is great spot for a picnic.

'Drífandi' means 'Ambitious', which is perhaps in reference to the poet rather than the height of the waterfall, although the latter is considerable (but not measured). There is also a cave in the area called Gluggaból ('Window Cave'). Very nearby, there are two other interesting waterfalls, Þórðarfoss and Gluggafoss (see the previous entry).

Directions

From the town of Hvolsvöllur, drive east on Route 261 (Fljótshlíðarvegur) for 16.5 km, past a farm entrance, to where a sign indicates Þorsteinslundur. Drive to the parking area at the end of the track. Go through the gate and across the farm track into the park. Follow the path and you will soon come across the waterfall.

Drífandi falls down the moss-covered rock face, dancing in the breeze. GPS: 63°43'17" N 19°54'34" W (63.72139, -19.90944)

Ægissíðufoss (Ægissufoss)

Region:	Suðurland (coastal)	Facing:	SW	
Town:	Hella	Tiers:	2	
Area:	Rangarvellir	Height:	★	1+2 m
River:	Ytri-Rangá	Width:	★★★★★	58 m
GPS:	63°49'09.5" N 20°25'00.2" W	Scenery:	★★★	
(deg dec)	63.819299, -20.416735	Access:	2WD	Drive-up

Description

Ægissíðufoss is one of Iceland's many low, broad waterfalls on salmon rivers. Its stepped and cut-up form renders it quite picturesque, but this is likely to vary a lot with the seasons, and rainfall may cause water levels to rise and submerge the rocks. There is a fish ladder on one side, and it is a favourite spot for many salmon anglers.

Directions

From the town of Hella, take Route 1 north-west for 800 m then turn south onto Route 25 (Þykkvabæjarvegur). Drive for 2.7 km then turn left onto a gravel road where a sign indicates Ægissíðufoss. It is 400 m to the end of the road and the parking area. You get a pretty good view from the parking area but it is only 150 m to reach the water's edge.

Ægissíðufoss with salmon ladder and angler. GPS: 63°49'9" N 20°25'5" W (63.81917, -20.41806)

Urriðafoss

Region:	Suðurland (coastal)	Facing:	S		
Town:	Selfoss	Tiers:	1		
Area:	Flói	Height:	★ ½	4-6 m	
River:	Þjórsá	Width:	★★★★★★	220 m	
GPS:	63°55'29.7" N 20°40'19.4" W	Scenery:	★★★★ ½		
(deg dec)	63.924905, -20.672050	Access:	2WD	Drive-up	

Description

Urriðafoss ('Salmon Falls') may not be very high but it is certainly amazing. It is a fabulous waterfall. It boasts the highest volume of water of any waterfall in Iceland, rising from an average of 350 m³/s to 1500 m³/s in spring. The falls cover an enormous breadth of up to 220 m, although a good portion is partially blocked by three large rock outcrops that channel the bulk of the flow down two raging chutes. There is a deep V-shaped channel behind a smaller rock in the centre chute. This creates much of the turbulence that makes this waterfall so fascinating.

Photographs do not do Urriðafoss justice, it is so broad and low, but it is one of the most beautiful waterfalls in Iceland. However, this beauty is in danger of being sacrificed to the needs of hydroelectric power generation. Landsvirkjunn, the National Power Company of Iceland has proposed the construction of a 130 MW power plant at Urriðafoss. The realization would greatly diminish the flow of the waterfall, to the extent that it might almost disappear. These plans for harvesting the river highlight the conflict between nature conservation principles and the profitable utilisation of nature's energy resources. There is fierce resistance by those who wish to preserve the waterfall in all its splendour, and perhaps it is in support of this that there is a 200 m viewing area that is very well managed and roped off, complete with an information panel providing information on the waterfall, its history, and possibly very diminished future.

As might be expected from the waterfall's name, salmon are known to leap the falls and venture higher upriver. Also, seals can sometimes be seen below the rocks, where they come to feast on the fish.

Directions

From the roundabout in the centre of Selfoss, drive east on Route 1 towards Hvolsvöllur for 18 km, past the junction for Route 30, then turn south onto Route 302 (Urriðafossvegur) just before the bridge over the Þjórsá. There is a sign for Urriðafoss. Continue another 2 km, past the farm having the same name, then turn left where a sign indicates the parking area for the waterfall. A short path leads to the viewing area, although you have a good perspective of the falls from the car park.

Urriðafoss extends over 200 m across the Þjórsá. It is a magnificent waterfall. GPS: 63°55'26" N 20°40'25" W (63.92389, -20.67361)

Raging waters as the Þjórsá is channelled between the rocks. GPS: 63°55'26" N 20°40'25" W (63.92389, -20.67361)

Faxi (Vatnsleysufoss, Faxafoss, Fossin Faxi)

Region:	Suðurland (central)	Facing:	NW	
Town:	Reykholt	Tiers:	1	
Area:	Biskupstungur	Height:	★★	7 m
River:	Tungufljót	Width:	★★★★★	90 m
GPS:	64°13'30.2" N 20°20'12.4" W	Scenery:	★★★	
(deg dec)	64.225070, -20.336773	Access:	2WD	Drive-up

Description

Faxi, or Vatnsleysufoss as it is often shown on road maps, also goes by the names of Faxafoss or Fossin Faxi. This is a different Faxi from the one near the Laugarfell Highland Hostel. This Faxi is located on the 'Golden Circle' the popular tourist route going out from Reyjavik and is virtually within a large, open and picturesque campsite.

Faxi seems to spring from nowhere in otherwise flat, fertile plains and farmland. It is not very high, but nevertheless quite imposing. A large volume of turbulent water drops down 7 m or so, spread over a slight arc, 90 m wide. There is a fish ladder on the north side. A small channel bypasses the waterfall on the south side going round an island to drop down and rejoin the Tungufljót a little further downstream.

Directions

From the centre of Reykholt, drive north-east on Route 35 (Biskupstungnabraut) for 7.3 km. There will be a road on the right and a small sign for a restaurant saying 'Við Faxa'. Take the road for less than 100 m to a parking area overlooking the falls. There is a lovely view from there and from the restaurant nearby, where there is a short path leading to a viewing deck, but you should wander around a little. You can reach the river bank very easily from within the campsite.

Faxi, viewed from the overlook. GPS: 64°13'33" N 20°20'18" W (64.22583, -20.33833)

Brúarárfoss (Brúarfoss)

Region:	Suðurland (central)	Facing:	SE	
Town:	Laugarvatn	Tiers:	1	
Area:	Laugardalur	Height:	★	
River:	Brúará	Width:	★ ★ ★ ★	
GPS:	64°15'51.8" N 20°30'57.9" W	Scenery:	★ ★ ★ ★	
(deg dec)	64.264399, -20.516095	Access:	2WD	Easy

Description

Brúarárfoss derives its name from a natural stone arch that once existed over the river near the waterfall. According to legend, a Skálholt diocese employee destroyed the bridge in 1602, at the time of a great famine in Iceland. He wanted to prevent the hungry peasants coming to Skálholt for food. The man is said to have drowned himself in the river some time later. 'Brúarárfoss' roughly means 'Bridge Falls' but a more correct translation is probably 'The waterfall on the river with a bridge'.

Brúarárfoss is very photogenic. The Brúará broadens out in this area into a shallow expanse, barely covering uneven bedrock. A channel has formed in in the middle and water flows into it as a low, long U-shaped cascade. The bright blueness of the water contrasts starkly with the black bedrock and mossy, mottled-green rocks.

You can see two other waterfalls on the Brúará. From the parking area you can follow the little stream down to the river where you will join a trail going to Miðfoss, 900 m below Brúarárfoss. Hlauptungufoss is 700 m further on.

Directions

From Laugarvatn take Route 37 (Laugarvatnsvegur) north and west. Pass the junction with Route 355 and drive 1.9 km. Turn left onto Rekyjavegur road into the Brekkuskógur housing complex. Follow the road as it turns to the left and right, then continue until the end where there is a small parking area. It is about a 1-minute walk to a small footbridge over a little stream, then another 4 minutes along a trail to the waterfall.

Brúarárfoss, its blue waters and dark, mossy rocks. GPS: 64°15'51" N 20°30'56" W (64.26417, -20.51556)

Gullfoss

Region:	Suðurland (central)	Facing:	S-W		
Town:	Reykholt	Tiers:	2		
Area:	Tunguheidi	Height:	★★★★	11+20 m	
River:	Hvítá	Width:	★★★★★★		
GPS:	64°19'36.1" N 20°07'15.3" W	Scenery:	★★★★★		
(deg dec)	64.326687, -20.120931	Access:	2WD	Easy	

Description

Ah, Gullfoss, mighty Gullfoss! The very name evokes the atmosphere of Iceland. It is certainly the most famous of its waterfalls. It is vast, it is gargantuan, it is magnificent, it is astounding. It merits everything that is said about it. While many waterfalls owe their beauty to the surrounding scenery, Gullfoss _is_ the scenery.

Gullfoss is formed as the glacial river Hvítá ('White River') drops over two hard ledges of basalt lava. The upper falls face south, stretching diagonally across the river, and are 11 m high and around 200 m wide. Immediately afterwards, the lower falls turn 90° to the right and drop a further 20 m into a narrow gorge that runs parallel to the ledge.

The Hvítá carries a huge quantity of water from its source, Lake Hvítávatn. The average volume is about 109 m³/s but can reach over 2000 m³/s. At times of flash flooding the gorge below the waterfall has even overflowed. (The Hvítá later combines with three other rivers, the Tungufljót, the Brúará and the Stóra-Laxá, doubling the volume of the river. Just north of the town of Selfoss it meets the Sog River where it becomes the Ölfusá, the most voluminous river in Iceland, which then flows into the Atlantic Ocean.)

'Gullfoss' means 'Golden Falls', but the origin of the name is unclear. There are three theories. The first is that it comes from the golden hue of the waters in the evening. The second is from the golden rainbow that often appears when the sun shines on the abundant spray. The last, and the most poetic, theory comes from Sveinn Pálsson's travel journal, which relates a story about a farmer named Gýgur who lived at Gýgjarhóll near the river. Gýgur could not bear the thought of someone else taking his gold after his death, so he put it into a chest and threw it into the waterfall.

Gullfoss and the surrounding area were designated a protected reserve in 1979 after a dispute about utilizing the falls to generate electricity. Not surprisingly, there are many facilities for the thousands of tourists who flock there every year. The visitor site on the west side of Gullfoss has extensive parking and is very well managed. There is an excellently maintained path and staircase to reach different viewpoints at and above the falls.

Very few sightseers venture to the east side of Gullfoss, although the views are no less impressive than on the other side – when the spray is not drenching you and getting in your eyes. From the ridge overlooking Gullfoss, you get a head-on view of the upper falls, and it is a remarkable sight. However, it takes more effort to get there, and the area is left in its natural state.

Directions

For the touristic, west side of Gullfoss:

From Reykjavik, it is about a 2-hour drive. Take Route 1 north towards Mosfelsbær, then drive east on Route 36 (Þingvallavegur). When you get to Þingvellir turn south onto Route 361 (Vallavegur), which then merges once again with Route 36. Follow the signs for Geysir and Gullfoss, taking Routes 365 (Lyngdalsheiðarvegur), then Route 37 (Laugarvatnsvegur), and finally Route 35 (Biskupstungnabraut). Continue past the also very-visited Geysir to Gullfoss. The first entrance takes you to the lower parking area. This is closest to the falls. The upper parking area is 500 m along Route 35. This is closest to the tourist facilities and the trail along the ridge overlooking the falls. If you are coming from Reykholt, drive north-east on Route 35 (Biskupstungnabraut) past Geysir to Gullfoss.

For the east side of Gullfoss:

Starting at the west side of Gullfoss, take Route 35 (Biskupstungnabraut) south-east, then turn onto Route 30 (Skeiða- og Hrunamannavegur) a few kilometres before Geysir. Continue to the junction with Route 349 (Tungufellsvegur) where you will turn left and drive for 2.3 km. At this point, bear right on Hrunamannaafréttur for 5.5 km until you come to a sign for Gullfoss. Turn left and follow the track for 700 m to a small parking area with an information panel.

There is a vague trail of about 1 km across the heath to the waterfall, but it is sometimes marked, sometimes not, and is bushy and rocky so give yourself 25 minutes. If you lose sight of the path just head towards the clouds of spray. Since the trail disappears from time to time, coming back will probably take longer due to the lack of reference points and any indication of where you parked. If you do not pay attention on your outwards trek, you could find yourself hunting about, looking for where you originally started.

The upper falls of Gullfoss, seen from the east side of the river. If you look very carefully, you might just be able to see a dot that is a man on the viewing platform on the far left. GPS: 64°19'35" N 20°7'10" W (64.32639, -20.11944)

Gullfoss drops in two steps at right angles to one another. GPS: 64°19'34" N 20°7'28" W (64.32611, -20.12444)

A view from the upper path on the west side, looking along the first tier. GPS: 64°19'34" N 20°7'28" W (64.32611, -20.12444)

Nýjifoss

Region:	Suðurland (central)	Facing:	SE	
Town:	Reykholt	Tiers:	4	
Area:	Lake Hagavatn	Height:	★★★★	
River:	Far (Farið)	Width:	★★★	
GPS:	64°28'38.4" N 20°15'16.8" W	Scenery:	★★★★	
(deg dec)	64.477324, -20.254675	Access:	4WD/SUV	Easy

Description

Nýjifoss is a unique, quadruple-tiered waterfall in the highlands, very close to the Langjökull glacier, the second largest ice cap in Iceland. Together the four tiers drop about 50 m (5+10+15+20 m) over a distance of about 115 m. The width varies from 1 to about 15 m. Nýjifoss is not on a river but emanates directly from Lake Hagavatn, itself formed by glacial melt, and then flows out as the river Far, also called Farið.

Nýjifoss is sometimes incorrectly called Leynifoss. In fact the latter was a different waterfall that became obstructed by geological changes within the last century. The lake then overflowed and created a new outlet that is now Nýjifoss ('New Falls').

This is a fascinating waterfall to see, quite literally on several levels. At the base, you have a view of the lowest two tiers as they drop into a shallow pool and flow out as the newly formed river. You need to climb up the slopes to see the upper two tiers and the lake that pours into them. The views from the top are wonderful, with Lake Hagavatn on one side and the barren desert-like landscape with the river winding through it, on the other.

Directions

Starting from Gullfoss, drive north on Route 35 (Biskupstungnabraut). Continue for about 11.3 km and take Route F335 (Hagavatnsvegur) to the left. There is a signpost saying 'Hagavatn 15 km' (the actual distance is closer to 16 km). Although this is a road designated for 4WD vehicles, it is passable with a high clearance SUV (at your own risk), as far as a major ford, about 14 km down the track. You will cross two small streams along the way. If you have an SUV, you need to park here, wade across the river and hike the remaining 2 km distance to the waterfall. Otherwise, it is a rough 4WD track to the falls, crossing several areas of shallow water.

You can walk up to the falls for a good view of the lowest two tiers, and can even approach them closely. Do not miss the upper tiers and the sight of the lake. It is about a 250 m climb following an indistinct trail up the hill for the best views.

The lowest two tiers of Nýjifoss. GPS: 64°28'34" N 20°15'13" W (64.47611, -20.25361)

Lake Hagavatn and the upper two tiers of Nýjifoss. GPS: 64°28'39" N 20°15'17" W (64.47750, -20.25472)

Gýgjarfoss (Gígjufoss)

Region:	Suðurland (central)	Facing:	NW		
Town:	Reykholt	Tiers:	1		
Area:	Kjölur	Height:	★ ★		
River:	Jökulkvísl	Width:	★ ★ ★ ★		
GPS:	64°42'12.0" N 19°23'49.2" W	Scenery:	★ ★ ★ ½		
(deg dec)	64.703333, -19.396997	Access:	2WD	Drive-up	

Description

Gýgjarfoss is located high up in the highlands, about 60 km north-east of Gullfoss. It is a fascinating waterfall arising at the confluence of the Jökulkvísl and the smaller Blákvisl, which descends from the Hofsjökull glacier. It is around 6 m in height with turbulent waters, a convoluted form, and a width extending to about 40 m. A small gorge of looming black rock at its exit adds mystery to the falls. You can view Gýgjarfoss from a wide variety of positions and perspectives, and you should take your time to wander around to admire it.

Just getting to Gýgjarfoss is worth the effort. From Gullfoss the road winds its way through spectacular landscapes, with views of Lake Hvítárvatn (the source for Gullfoss) and the Sólkatla and Kerlingarfjöll mountains in the distance.

Gýgjarfoss can be translated as 'Ogress Falls' from the archaic word 'Gýgur' for 'Troll Woman'. There are two other waterfalls, Tröllkonufoss and Skessufoss, that have roughly the same meaning, yet have very different origins. Another waterfall, Tröllafoss, has the more generic name for Troll Falls.

Directions

Starting from Gullfoss, drive north for about 60 km along Route 35 (Biskupstungnabraut). You will eventually reach the junction where Route 35 becomes F35 and F347 branches off to the right. Gýgjarfoss is about 4 km south-west from the junction, on F347 (Kerlingarfjallavegur). Although this is a road designated for 4WD vehicles only, it is easily passable with 2WD cars as far as the waterfall. You will reach the waterfall just before the ford crossing the rivers. There is ample parking and it is only about 100 m to the falls.

Gýgjarfoss is formed where the clear waters of the river Blákvisl merge with the muddier Jökulkvísl. GPS: 64°42'12" N 19°23'46" W (64.70333, -19.39611)

Þjófafoss

Region:	Suðurland (central)	Facing:	N		
Town:	Flúðir	Tiers:	1		
Area:	Þjórsárdalur , Landsveit	Height:	★ ★	4-12 m
River:	Þjórsá	Width:	★ ★ ★ ★	30-50 m
GPS:	64°03'24.3" N 19°52'00.1" W	Scenery:	★ ★ ★ ½	
(deg dec)	64.056742, -19.866704	Access:	2WD	Drive-up

Description

The Þjórsá is the longest river in Iceland, with a volume only exceeded by that of the Ölfusá. Þjófafoss ('Thieves Falls') is one of the many notable waterfalls along this river.

The height, width and colour of the water can vary considerably as the Þjórsá is dammed a little further upriver. Naturally, this affects the water flow over Þjófafoss. In the winter months, the height may be as much as 12 m when the flow is low, with a width reduced to around 30 m. This is compensated for, however, by the lack of silt in the water, which takes on an almost fluorescent turquoise or teal colour. When the water flow is maximal, after a lot of rain, or during peak melting of the glaciers, the silt turns the water a muddy brown and the height can be reduced to as little as 4 m as the river level rises, with a width extending to 50 m or more.

Although the surrounding landscape is a shallow canyon in a flat, volcanic plain, Þjófafoss is a beautiful waterfall and the view with Búrfell Mountain behind it is very picturesque. If you drive just 2 km north, you can see 250 m wide Tröllkonufoss, also known as Tröllkonuhlaup.

Directions

From the roundabout in the centre of Selfoss, take Route 1 east for 29 km or, alternatively, if you are coming from the town of Hella drive west on Route 1 for 7.3 km. Turn north onto Route 26 (Landvegur) and drive for 44 km. At this point, turn left where you will see a signpost for Þjófafoss. Continue along the gravel road for 3.7 km to a wide pull-out area, and park. A short 50 m walk leads to a view above Þjófafoss.

Þjófafoss at a time of peak water flow. The volcano Hekla is in the distance. GPS: 64°3'25" N 19°52'7" W (64.05694, -19.86861)

Hjálparfoss

Region:	Suðurland (central)	Facing:	S-SW		
Town:	Flúðir	Tiers:	1		
Area:	Þjórsárdalur	Height:	★★	9 m	
River:	Fossá	Width:	★★★★	12+22 m	
GPS:	64°06'57.1" N 19°50'58.9" W	Scenery:	★★★ ½		
(deg dec)	64.115867, -19.849705	Access:	2WD	Drive-up	

Description

About 13 km downstream, as the crow flies, from the grand Háifoss lies Hjálparfoss. This much-visited waterfall sits in the Vikrar lava fields north of the volcano Hekla, near the confluence of the Fossá and the Þjórsá. The name derives from the surrounding area, called Hjalp ('Help'), because travellers crossing the highland plateau of Sprengisandur found the vegetation helpful to graze their horses after the long journey in the barren interior.

Hjálparfoss's uniqueness comes from its position where the Fossá recombines after splitting and flowing around an island in the middle of the river. About one third of the flow drops over a ledge on the west side and the other two thirds over a ledge, twice as wide, on the east. The waters collect in a large pool within a circular basin before flowing out through a channel to the south. The surrounding jagged and very convoluted rock formations are some of the most interesting columnar basalt examples in Iceland.

Directions

From Selfoss, take Route 30 (Skeiða-og Hrunamannavegur) north — or from Flúðir, the same route south — to the junction with Route 32 (Þjórsárdalsvegur). Drive on Route 32 for about 31.5 km. Turn right at the signpost for Hjálparfoss. The turnoff is about 100 m before a bridge over the river. Follow the road for 1 km to its end, where there is a large parking area with picnic tables overlooking the falls.

You have a good view of Hjálparfoss from the picnic area, but a short stroll down the steps and managed path to the pool will provide you with some lovely viewpoints from a variety of angles.

Hjálparfoss, viewed from the front of the pool. GPS: 64°6'55" N 19°51'6" W (64.11528, -19.85167)

Gjárfoss (Gjáfoss)

Region:	Suðurland (central)	Facing:	SW		
Town:	Flúðir	Tiers:	2		
Area:	Gjáskógar in Þjórsárdalur	Height:	★★★	16 m	
River:	Rauðá	Width:	★	3 m	
GPS:	64°09'04.6" N 19°44'11.9" W	Scenery:	★★★		
(deg dec)	64.151285, -19.736645	Access:	2WD	Easy	

Description

Gjáin is a charming, luscious, green valley nestling in a hollow of an otherwise barren landscape. Gjárfoss ('Gorge Falls') is one of two prominent waterfalls dropping into the valley (the other being Gjáinfoss — see the next entry). It is fed by a small stream, the Rauðá, which is in turn fed by several springs upstream. Although Gjárfoss is insubstantial in both height and volume it is very attractive, having a unique appearance and lovely setting. Here, the Rauðá is forced to split around a prominent rock before recombining as it slips over a ledge and drops in two jumps into a deep turquoise-blue pool.

While Gjárfoss is lovely, it undoubtedly owes most of its attractiveness to the surrounding Gjáin valley of which it is a part. It is the beauty of the area that makes the visit so worthwile. Gjárfoss and Gjáinfoss are on two different streams that combine at a picturesque set of low-lying cascades. With its sculptured contours and mingling waters, the valley seems to have been pulled from some imaginary Tolkien-like fairy tale.

Only a kilometre to the east of the valley, and near where you are likely to have parked your vehicle, is the historical Þjóðveldisbærinn Stöng (Stöng Commonwealth Farm), a reconstructed Viking-era farmstead. It is a historically accurate reconstruction of the three buildings, including a longhouse, which stood 7 km to the north at Stöng. The farm was buried under volcanic ash in 1104 following the eruption of the volcano Hekla.

Directions

From Selfoss, take Route 30 (Skeiða-og Hrunamannavegur) north — or from Flúðir, the same route south — to the junction with Route 32 (Þjórsárdalsvegur). Drive on Route 32 for about 32 km, and after crossing the bridge over the Fossá turn left onto Route 327 (Stangarvegur). This is the road to Stöng farm. Drive for a further 5.7 km and park in the parking area for the farm. If you have a 4WD vehicle, you can cross the river at the ford and park on the other side.

If you parked on the south of the river, cross the river via the footbridge. From there, or from the car park on the other (north) side of the river, take the trail that follows the river upstream (do not take the path that climbs upwards to the farm). It is about 800 m to the Gjáin valley and a view over Gjárfoss.

To get to the south side of the valley you need to wade across the stream or follow the directions for Gjáinfoss.

Gjárfoss, viewed from the north side of the valley. GPS: 64°09'03.7" N 19°44'14.7" W (64.15103, -19.73742)

No other waterfall resembles Gjárfoss. GPS: 64°9'4" N 19°44'15" W (64.15111, -19.73750)

Gjáinfoss

Region:	Suðurland (central)	Facing:	SW		
Town:	Flúðir	Tiers:	1		
Area:	Gjáskógar in Þjórsárdalur	Height:	★★	12 m	
River:	Unknown	Width:	★	3+2 m	
GPS:	64°09'01.9" N 19°44'04.8" W	Scenery:	★★★		
(deg dec)	64.150526, -19.734666	Access:	2WD	Easy	

Description

Gjáinfoss may not be the proper name of this waterfall, if it has a name at all (the stream that feeds it is also unnamed). But Gjáinfoss seems to be the most appropriate name for the second of the two main waterfalls in the Gjáin valley. Although not anywhere nearly as attractive as Gjárfoss, Gjáinfoss has its own character. Like Gjárfoss, it is really the beauty of the entire valley that makes the visit so worthwhile.

Directions

From Gjárfoss: If you have a 2WD vehicle, you will need to leave it there and walk to Gjáin along a 1 km trail that follows the south bank of the stream. If you have a 4WD vehicle, you can continue driving up the road on the south side of the river, now F327, for another 1.4 km, at which point you need to fork left, to a loop and a parking area that overlooks the valley. The road is designated for 4WD vehicles only, but it is passable with a high clearance SUV, at your own risk.

From the east: If you have a 4WD vehicle, or high clearance SUV, you can also reach Gjáin from the east. From Route 32 (Þjórsárdalsvegur) take the turn onto Route 332 (Háafossvegur) where there is a signpost for Hólaskogur. About 550 m along the road there is an intersection with Route 327 (Stangarvegur, which shortly becomes F327). The intersection is signposted for Gjáin.

From the parking area overlooking Gjáin, take the stairs and steep path down into the valley. Gjáinfoss is at the east end but you can wander about on several trails.

The Gjáin valley, viewed from the south side, with Gjárfoss on the left and Gjáinfoss on the right. GPS: 64°8'58" N 19°44'16" W (64.14944, -19.73778)

Háifoss

Region:	Suðurland (central)	Facing:	SE		
Town:	Flúðir	Tiers:	1		
Area:	Fossárdalur in Þjórsárdalur	Height:	★ ★ ★ ★ ★	122 m	
River:	Fossá	Width:	★ ★	12 m	
GPS:	64°12'28.6" N 19°41'13.1" W	Scenery:	★ ★ ★ ★ ★		
(deg dec)	64.207931, -19.686983	Access:	2WD	Easy	

Description

The view of Háifoss is spellbinding. It is considered to be the third tallest waterfall in Iceland after Morsárfoss and Glymur. It stems from the same river Fossá (yes, yet another river named Fossá), as does Hjálparfoss further downstream, and for such a magnificent waterfall it is a shame that the river was not named something a little grander. This Fossá is a quite substantial river that drains from a high mountain plateau. It splits into two channels about 800 m before Háifoss with the second channel dropping off the ledge as the waterfall Granni (see the next entry), just 200 m away to the north-east. Both Háifoss and Granni pour into the valley Fossárdalur; where their waters recombine. The Fossá later runs into the river Þjorsá.

Háifoss plummets 122 m in a largely uninterrupted plunge into a boulder-strewn pool, which is almost obscured by a billowing cloud of spray, accompanied by a satisfying, perpetual roar that echoes down the canyon. When you see Háifoss, you get two of Iceland's tallest waterfalls for the price of one, as Granni is part of the picture. While there are many tall, thin streams in Iceland, Háifoss and Granni have ample water flow, and it is the combination of the two falls, with height, volume and the magnificent, rugged canyon that makes Háifoss (and Granni) so spectacular.

'Háifoss' not surprisingly translates as 'High Falls', although the Icelandic pronunciation is not what an English speaker might expect from the spelling. It is pronounced more like 'How-i-foss'. Also surprising is that it is only comparatively recently, late in the twentieth century, that the waterfall was bestowed with this name.

Directions

From Selfoss, take Route 30 (Skeiða- og Hrunamannavegur) north — or from Flúðir, the same route south — to the junction with Route 32 (Þjórsárdalsvegur). Drive on Route 32 for about 43 km, past the turnoff to Stöng, to Route 332 (Háafossvegur). There is a signpost for Hólaskogur, but none for Háifoss at the junction; although you will find one 550 m up the road where Route 332 intersects with Route F327 (Stangarvegur) that loops around from Gjáin and Stöng. Bear right and continue along the same road. It becomes quite rough but is passable by 2WD vehicles. After 6.6 km, turn left at the sign for Háifoss and drive another 500 m to the parking area.

If you are coming from Stöng and Gjain and have a 4WD vehicle, take the 4WD road, F327, until it intersects with Route 332. It is passable with a high-clearance SUV, at your own risk.

From the parking area, there is an easy 500 m trail to the main viewpoint on a small rocky promontory. Take the time to walk back and forth along the canyon rim for many wonderful views of the waterfalls and the canyon itself. For the very adventurous, it is possible to reach the base of Háifoss by hiking a distance of about 8 km from Stöng (see the entry for Gjáinfoss).

Háifoss and Granni, and the magnificent canyon of Fossárdalur. GPS: 64°12'19" N 19°41'7" W (64.20528, -19.68528)

Fossárdalur, seen from close to Granni. The spray from Háifoss is just visible. GPS: 64°12'30" N 19°40'53" W (64.20833, -19.68139)

Granni (Grannifoss)

Region:	Suðurland (central)	Facing:	E	
Town:	Flúðir	Tiers:	2	
Area:	Fossárdalur in Þjórsárdalur	Height:	★★★★★ ½	
River:	Fossá	Width:	★★	
GPS:	64°12'33.1" N 19°40'59.4" W	Scenery:	★★★★	
(deg dec)	64.209192, -19.683163	Access:	2WD	Easy

Description

When you go to see Háifoss you get Granni thrown in too. This makes for a wonderful view, but poor old Granni gets no respect. The name, meaning 'Neighbour', even suggests its status as second billing to the more famous waterfall about 200 m to the south-west.

Granni does not seem to have an officially recorded height, but it is close to that of Háifoss. The main chute drops about 100 m in two steps down into the canyon, of which it forms the head. It is preceded by a series of cascades over small ledges, before a sharp bend and the falls proper.

Directions

Follow the directions for Háifoss. Although you get many different views of Granni along with those of Háifoss, you need to hike north-west over the heath to get close and admire Granni alone. There is no trail, but it is easy to get close to the rim where you can also get a wonderful view down the canyon to the south.

Due to its situation at the head of the ravine, and at 90° to it, Granni is often shaded by the canyon walls, so the best time to see it is from mid-morning to midday.

Granni forms the head of the Fossárdalur canyon. GPS: 64°12'25" N 19°40'57" W (64.20694, -19.68250)

Sigöldufoss (Sigoldafoss, Hnubbafossar)

Region:	Suðurland (central)	Facing:	N-NW		
Town:	Flúðir	Tiers:	1		
Area:	Krókslón	Height:	★★	10 m	
River:	Tungnaá	Width:	★★★★	30-50 m	
GPS:	64°10'12.5" N 19°07'51.4" W	Scenery:	★★★★		
(deg dec)	64.170130, -19.130940	Access:	2WD	Easy	

Description

Easy to get to, yet unfortunately easily passed by, Sigöldufoss merits far more praise than its standard description of a modestly-sized waterfall leftover from the construction of a hydroelectric power plant. In fact, Sigöldufoss is a not-so-hidden gem of a waterfall that deserves lengthy admiration of its many facets and lustrous splendour.

The waterfall is on the remains of the river Tungnaá adjacent to the tailrace feeding the Sigöldustöð power station that takes most of the water from the reservoir of Lake Krókslón (the more generally used name for Lake Sigöldulón). At this point, the Tungnaá occupies a wide ledge that varies in width according to the amount of water allowed into the river. The ledge breaks into an irregular arc with the waterfall consisting of several minor sections, including a deep, central U-shaped channel, and a few large rocks that cause mayhem in the waters as they surge down into a tight channel. The width of the falls is nominally around 30 m but that does not adequately account for the convolutions of the river bank and the multiple sections.

Sigöldufoss is a waterfall that needs to be viewed from as many different places and angles as possible, and certainly from both sides of the river. While the north side is splendid and the most easily accessible, the south side is even more stunning. Adding to the beauty of the picture is the bright turquoise colour of the water, since the silt that would normally muddy the river has been left behind in the reservoir upriver. If you go back to either of the two bridges over the river Tungnaá and the outflow from the power station, you can get an interesting sight of the two flows combining, one a muddy brown and the other a crystalline turquoise blue.

Directions

From the south and west, take either Route 32 (Þjórsárdalsvegur) or 26 (Landvegur) to Route 208 (Skaftártunguvegur). The Sigöldustöð hydroelectric plant will be signposted. Continue for 5.5 km until you cross a bridge over the muddy outlow from the power station. Take the dirt road signposted for Sigöldufoss just after the bridge and before the next one over the Tungnaá. This will take you to the north side of the waterfall. Drive up and to the right for about 300 m to a parking area.

To get to the other side of the falls go back to the bridge, cross it and take an unsignposted dirt road 200 m south of it. Follow the track as it curves round to the left until you come to an area where you can park.

From either the north or south sides of the river, it is an easy walk to various viewing spots above the falls.

Sigöldufoss, viewed from the north side. GPS: 64°10'13" N 19°7'47" W (64.17028, -19.12972)

Sigöldufoss, viewed from the south side. GPS: 64°10'11" N 19°7'48" W (64.16972, -19.13000)

Ófærufoss

Region:	Suðurland (central)	Facing:	S	
Town:	Flúðir	Tiers:	3	
Area:	Eldgjá	Height:	★★★★	40 m
River:	Nyrðri-Ófæra	Width:	★★★	
GPS:	63°57'51.5" N 18°37'03.1" W	Scenery:	★★★★★	
(deg dec)	63.964309, -18.617519	Access:	4WD	Moderate

Description

Eldgjá contains the largest volcanic canyon in the world. The name Eldgjá is used for both the volcano and the canyon. The latter is a 40 km eruptive fissure, about 600 m wide, and up to 270 m deep. It last erupted in 934, with activity taking place along the whole extent of it. An estimated 18 km³ of magma poured out of the earth at that time. The lava-field is believed to cover 800 km², making it one of the most extensive lava fields on Earth since the last ice age.

The Nyrðri–Ófæra and Syðri–Ófæra, (Northern and Southern Impassable Rivers) flow through the Eldgjá canyon and join the river Skaftá. The northern river enters the rift as the magnificent waterfall Ófærufoss ('Impassable Falls').

The waterfall descends from the cliff top in two major tiers with a sloping, small series of ledges linking the two within a large open basin that comprises the third tier. The total height is around 40 m. The distinctive form, with the bowl-shaped central area and plumes of spray when the river is in full flood, is a majestic and breath-taking spectacle.

From Ófærufoss, you can walk another 5 km up to Gjátindur, which rises 943 m above sea level. There is a great view from the top. In addition, the waterfall Silfurfoss is not far away, off Route F208 and very close to the hostel at Hólaskjól (see the next entry).

Directions

Ófærufoss is located midway between the Landmannalaugar Nature Reserve and Kirkjubæjarklaustur.

From the north: Follow the direction for Sigöldufoss, then continue south on Route 208 (Skaftártunguvegur). After the bridges it becomes F208 and is only suitable for 4WD vehicles. Follow the road in the direction of Landmannalaugar. Drive past the intersection with F224 to Landmannalaugar and continue on F208. Go past the junction F208/F235 to a signposted turnoff for Eldgjá. The road is only passable for a few short summer months and you will need a good 4WD vehicle to cross a major ford on the way. You will arrive at a large parking area.

From Landmannalaugar: Take F224 (Landmannalaugavegur) north-east to F208 (Skaftártunguvegur), then go east and south, past the junction F208/F235 to the turnoff for Eldgjá and proceed as described above.

From the south: Take Route 208 (Skaftártunguvegur) east of Vik and west of Kirkjubæjarklaustur. You will pass through the Skaftártunga area, and into the Fjallabaksleið Nyrðri, where the road becomes F208 (also called by the latter name). Take the signposted turnoff to Eldgjá and proceed as described above.

From the parking area, a well-marked trail starts from a footbridge and goes about 2 km, leading to wooden steps and a viewing platform above the bottom tier of Ófærufoss. Although you can get a good view of the middle and top tiers from the platform in the best of conditions, at other times you may be drenched in spray.

Depending on the weather, the trail can be a little difficult with the almost immediate need to jump or wade across the fast-flowing river. You may need to contend with snow banks, boulders and flooded sand flats. To avoid wading across large puddles and streamlets, you may need to hike considerably past the waterfall to find a crossing point before doubling back on the other side. Assume up to an hour each way.

The three tiers of Ófærufoss. GPS: 63°57'49" N 18°37'1" W (63.96361, -18.61694)

Silfurfoss (Litli-Gullfoss, Huldufoss)

Region:	Suðurland (central)	Facing:	NE
Town:	Flúðir	Tiers:	1
Area:	Hánípugil	Height:	★★★
River:	Syðri-Ófæra	Width:	★★★
GPS:	63°54'26.1" N 18°36'41.0" W	Scenery:	★★★★
(deg dec)	63.907259, -18.611402	Access:	4WD/SUV/2WD Easy

Description

Silfurfoss is very near the hostel at Hólaskjól, which is located at the foot of the Lambaskarðshólar hills, at the edge of a lava field originating from the massive eruption in Eldgjá during the years 934 to 940 (see the previous entry). The waterfall seems to be officially unnamed but many call it Silfurfoss ('Silver Falls'). Since it resembles a smaller version of the well-known Gullfoss, it is often called Litli-Gullfoss ('Little Gullfoss'). However, locals like to call it Huldufoss ('Dark Falls').

Silfurfoss starts as a series of minor rapids then abruptly falls off a cliff into a narrow slot of a canyon at 90° to its flow. It plunges some 20 m, causing quite a noise and considerable spray. You can easily view it from a roped-off area just above the falls and from further downstream above the canyon.

Directions

From the south, take Route 208 (Skaftártunguvegur) east of Vik and west of Kirkjubæjarklaustur. You will pass through the Skaftártunga area, and into the Fjallabaksleið Nyrðri, where the road becomes F208 (also called by the latter name). This is a coarse gravel road, but in summer, it is passable by all types of vehicles. However, due to its 'F' designation, if you do not have a 4WD vehicle, you take it at your own risk. Hólaskjól is about 35 km from Route 1, and clearly signposted. There are no fords to cross along the way. Park at the hostel.

It is only a 350 m walk to the waterfall, up a path behind the hostel buildings at the south-eastern corner of the area.

Silfurfoss plunges into Hánípugil canyon. Note the man on the river bank.
GPS: 63°54'26" N 18°36'37" W (63.90722, -18.61028)

Index

This index of waterfalls, with page numbers, is in alphabetical order, disregarding accents for the convenience of those either unfamiliar with, or unsure of, the correct Icelandic spelling.

The ligature 'æ' is treated as 'ae', eth (Ð,ð) is transliterated as 'D,d', and thorn (Þ,þ) is treated as the last letter in the alphabet, i.e. following 'z'. Where alternative names and spelling of waterfalls are provided in the individual sections, they are also indexed here.